BRANCH LINES EAST OF NORWICH

The Wherry Lines

Richard Adderson and Graham Kenworthy

MP Middleton Press

Front cover: Class D16/3 4-4-0 no.62556 heads a mixed rake of coaches towards the coast in attractively wooded surroundings between Brundall Gardens Halt and Brundall on 7th April 1951. We are looking westwards, with Brundall Gardens Halt just out of sight round the curve in the distance. (B.Reading)

Rear cover: The wherry Albion is moored at Reedham Quay on the somewhat damp evening of 7th July 2009, as a class 170 rumbles over the swing bridge beyond. The ship was purchased by the Norfolk Wherry Trust in 1949, at a time when these vessels had all but disappeared from their native waterways. Her days of carrying general cargo are over, but she is a familiar sight on passenger charter voyages during the Summer months. The "Wherry Lines" marketing brand commemorates these distinctive vessels, which were once so familiar on the rivers which are never far from the railways covered in this book. This branding was introduced by British Rail for services between Norwich and Yarmouth/Lowestoft in the mid-1970s, and its use continued until the late 1980s. The title became dormant through the 1990s but was revived early in the 21st century as a significant marketing tool. (R.J.Adderson)

Readers of this book may be interested in the following society:

Great Eastern Railway Society,
J.R.Tant, Membership Secretary,
9 Clare Road,
Leytonstone,
London E11 1JU

Published February 2010
First reprint May 2012

ISBN 978 1 906008 69 7

© Middleton Press, 2010

Design Deborah Esher

Published by
    Middleton Press
    Easebourne Lane
    Midhurst
    West Sussex
    GU29 9AZ
Tel: 01730 813169
Fax: 01730 812601
Email: info@middletonpress.co.uk
www.middletonpress.co.uk

Printed in the United Kingdom by Henry Ling Limited, at the Dorset Press, Dorchester, DT1 1HD

CONTENTS

1.	Norwich Thorpe to Yarmouth Vauxhall	1- 61
2.	Yarmouth Tramway	62- 73
3.	Reedham Junction to Lowestoft	74-111
4.	Brundall Junction to Breydon Junction	112-120

INDEX

116	Acle	28	Cantley	36	Reedham
44	Berney Arms	82	Haddiscoe	74	Reedham Swing Bridge
49	Breydon Junction	112	Lingwood	91	Somerleyton
18	Brundall	102	Lowestoft Central	7	Whitlingham Junction
13	Brundall Gardens Halt	1	Norwich Thorpe	62	Yarmouth Tramway
24	Buckenham	97	Oulton Broad North	50	Yarmouth Vauxhall

ACKNOWLEDGEMENTS

In addition to those individuals acknowledged in the photographic credits, we are most grateful to G.Ashton, R.Green, G.Hawkins, G.Moore, J.Muter and A.Rush.

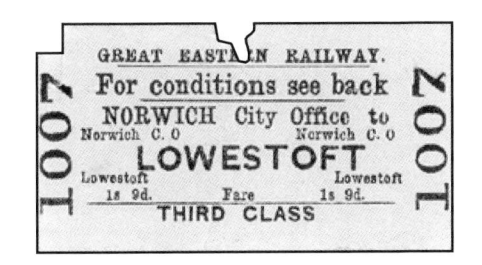

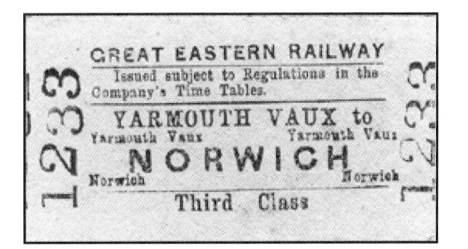

Railways of the area in 1954 showing pre-grouping ownerships.
Other maps in this volume are to a scale of 25 ins to 1 mile, unless otherwise stated.

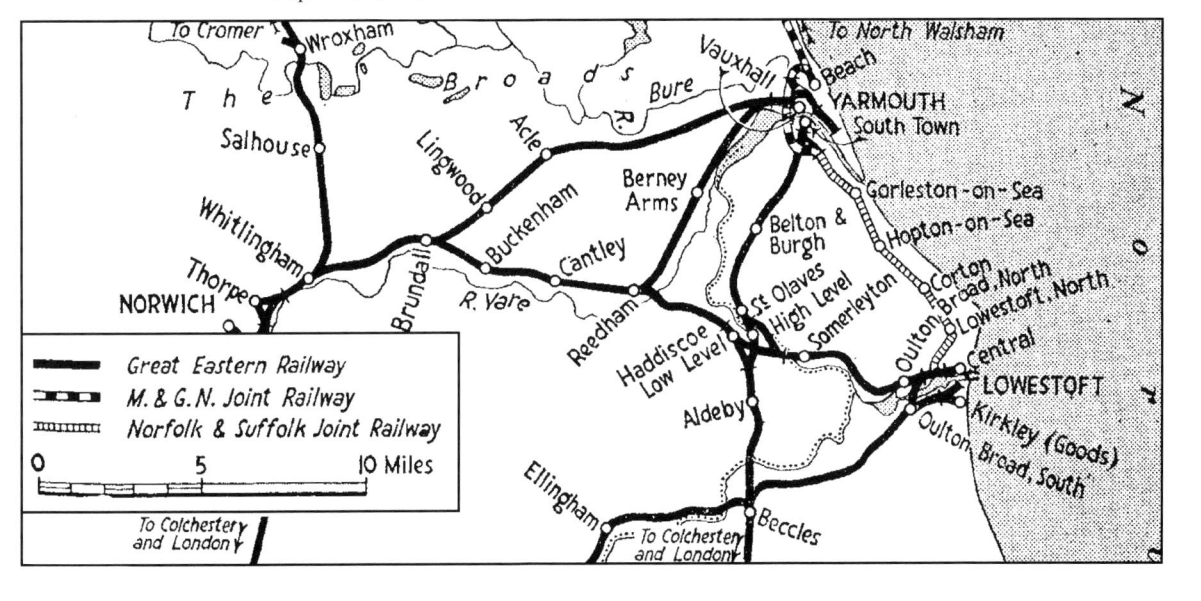

The 1946 edition is shown at 4 miles to 1 inch.

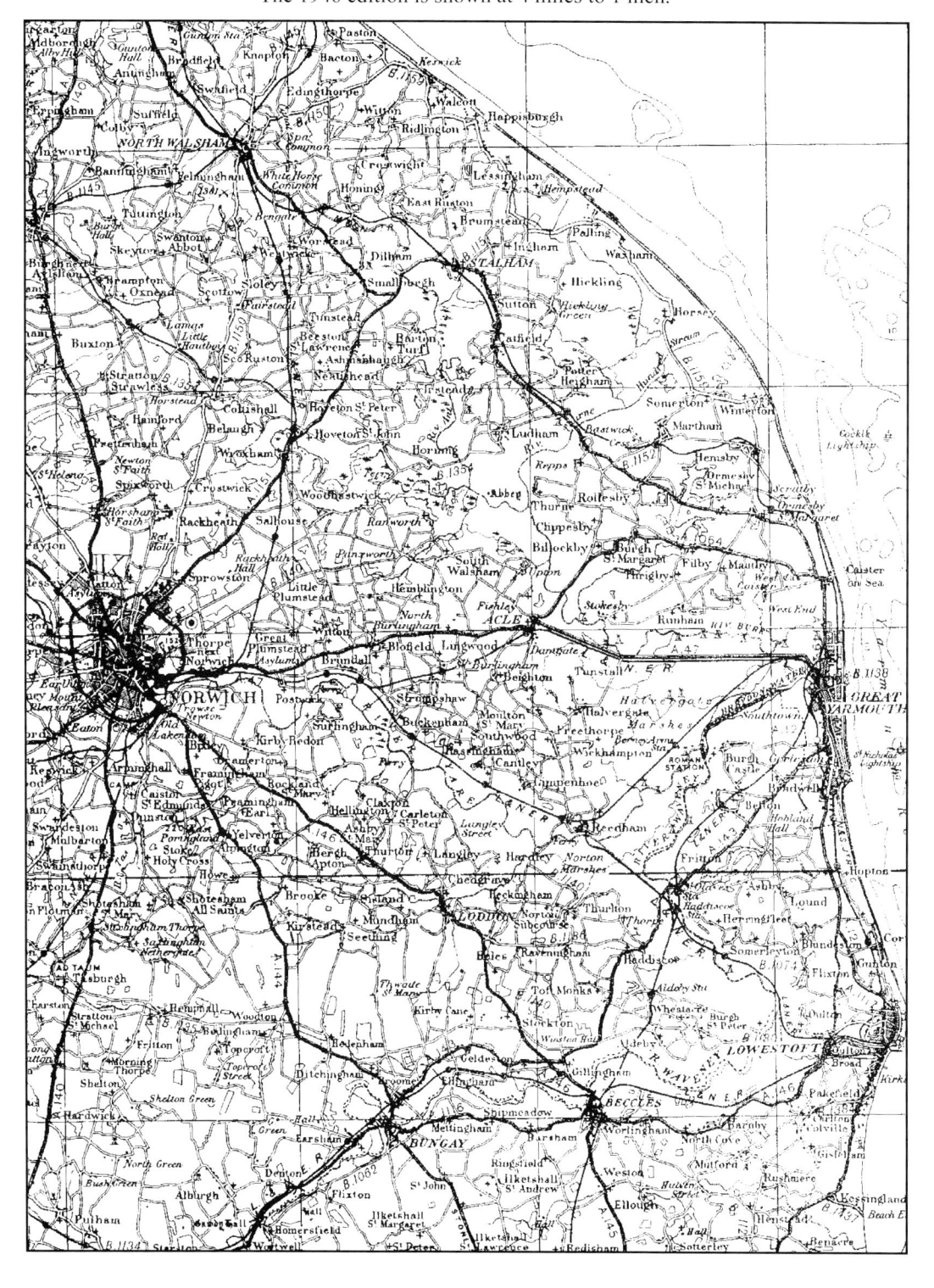

GEOGRAPHICAL SETTING

Norwich to Yarmouth via Reedham
To the east of Whitlingham Junction, between 2½ and 4½ miles from Norwich, the River Yare is diverted on a southward loop by an area of higher ground in the vicinity of the village of Postwick. The railway rises to negotiate a cutting through this finger of land. Apart from this rise and fall, the line is laid on the marshes which adjoin the northern bank of the river, and is virtually level all the way from Norwich to Yarmouth.

Yarmouth Tramway
Having crossed the River Bure outside Vauxhall station, the tramway headed south and followed the east bank of the River Yare for just over 1½ miles. At the foot of the approach road to the station, the tramway was joined by the Yarmouth Union line which was built to connect Yarmouth Beach station with the riverside quays. This route ran from a short distance north of Beach station and swung west to skirt the northern fringe of the town before turning south, via White Swan Yard to North Quay Junction.

Reedham to Lowestoft
Between the extremities of the branch, there are two cuttings, one at Reedham, between the station and the swing bridge, the other to the west of Oulton Broad. In both cases the route was laid out at a slightly higher level to keep excavations to a minimum. Apart from these "high" points and the need to gain height to cross Somerleyton Swing Bridge, most of the line runs across marshes, only slightly above sea level and never far from the rivers that empty into the North Sea at Yarmouth.

Brundall to Yarmouth via Acle
At Brundall Junction the line is at river level; around five miles further on, just beyond Acle, the line is again at river level, this time the River Bure. Between these two points, the line rises and falls about seventy feet, with Lingwood station located at the summit. East of Acle the line is almost level.

Mileages shown are from Liverpool St. via Cambridge and Norwich.

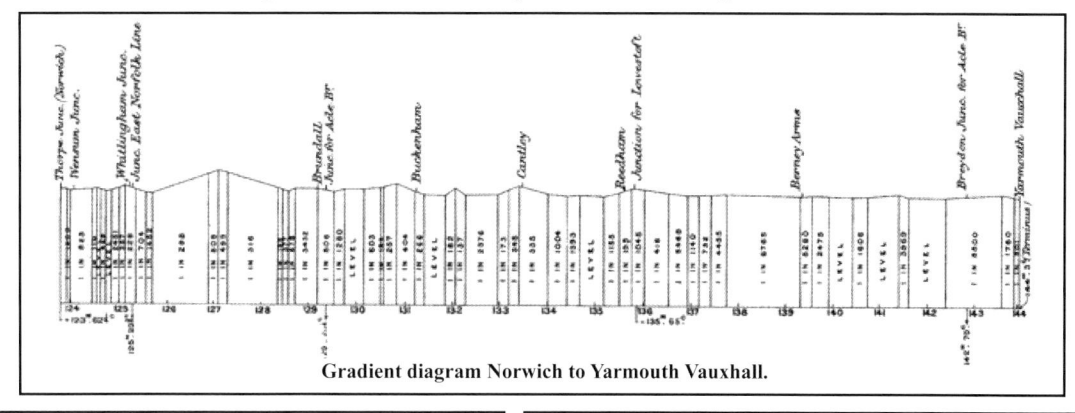

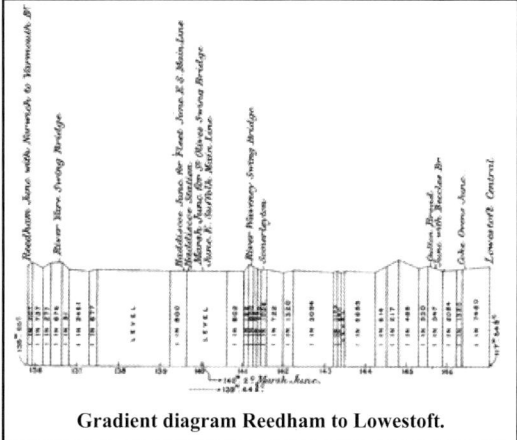

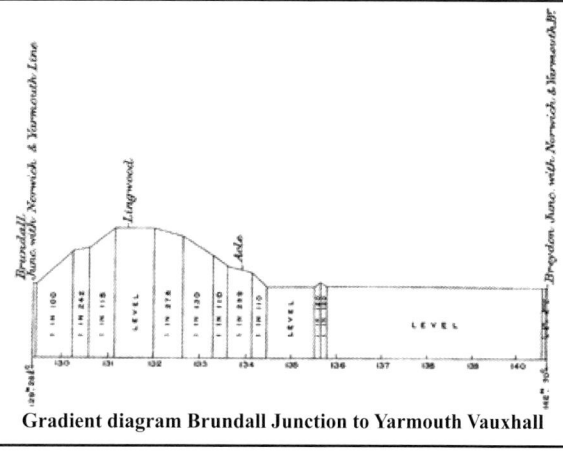

Gradient diagram Norwich to Yarmouth Vauxhall.

Gradient diagram Reedham to Lowestoft.

Gradient diagram Brundall Junction to Yarmouth Vauxhall.

HISTORICAL BACKGROUND

Norwich to Yarmouth via Reedham

The citizens and businessmen of Norwich had originally expected that their first experience of the railway age would arrive courtesy of the Eastern Counties Railway route from London via Colchester and Ipswich. However when it became obvious that this scheme was unlikely to penetrate beyond Colchester, the best hope for reviving the city's flagging economy lay with the scheme incorporated in 1842 as the Norfolk Railway, for a relatively simple route along the Yare Valley, connecting Norwich with the port of Yarmouth. Construction was fairly rapid and the line, single throughout, opened on 1st May 1844; it gained the distinction of being "The First Railway in Norfolk".

Following the opening of the branch from Reedham to Lowestoft in 1847, the section from Brundall to Reedham was doubled in 1849. The Norfolk Railway was leased to the Eastern Counties Railway in 1848, and both were, in turn, absorbed into the Great Eastern Railway on its formation in 1862.

The opening of the first section of the Cromer branch in 1874 led to the doubling of the Norwich (Thorpe Junction) to Whitlingham section in October of that year, while the line from the latter point to Brundall received similar improvement almost exactly one year later.

The Great Eastern Railway passed into the ownership of the London & North Eastern Railway on 1st January 1923, and the lines became part of the Eastern Region of British Railways upon nationalisation on 1st January 1948.

March 1967 saw the withdrawal of booking office facilities from all intermediate stations, ticket issue being dealt with subsequently by on-train conductor guards equipped with portable ticket machines.

On privatisation in 1997, services on the line became part of the Anglia Railways franchise, only to be taken over by **one** Railway in 2004, and rebranded National Express East Anglia in 2008.

All these post-1923 details also apply to the passenger lines that follow.

Yarmouth Tramway

The first access from Vauxhall station to North Quay, Hall Quay and South Quay was authorised by an 1847 Act and opened via a temporary bridge in the following year. Further extensions followed, particularly those resulting from an Act of 1866. Connection to these lines was achieved in 1882 by what became the Midland & Great Northern Joint company from its Beach station over the Yarmouth Union Railway via White Swan Yard to North Quay Junction at the foot of the incline from Vauxhall station. Traffic was horse drawn until the mid-1880s, after which, encouraged by the Borough Council, locomotive haulage was introduced. Despite this innovation, instructions relating to the use of horses were still issued as late as 1910.

The line saw considerable use in its lifetime but a variety of changes, particularly during the 1960s, led to a gradual decline, followed by complete closure at the end of 1975.

Reedham to Lowestoft

This was the earliest branch to connect Lowestoft to the national network. It owed its existence to the foresight and energies of Samuel Morton Peto who, in 1844, purchased the Norwich and Lowestoft Navigation Company. This company had been formed in the 1820s in an attempt to establish Lowestoft as an alternative to Yarmouth as the entry point for vessels to reach the inland port of Norwich. By the early 1840s, the company had become the victim of financial difficulties, and, with the opening of the railway between Norwich and Yarmouth via Reedham in 1844, Peto saw an opportunity for reviving the fortunes of the Suffolk port. The first step was taken when the Lowestoft Railway and Harbour Company was incorporated by an Act of June 1845 for a railway from Lowestoft to Reedham, and for improving the Harbour at Lowestoft.

The 11¼ mile single-track line was opened to goods traffic on 3rd May 1847 and to passengers a little under two months later, on 1st July, under the auspices of the Norfolk Railway Company which had taken over the railway and navigation from the Lowestoft Company in 1846.

Work on doubling the line between Reedham and Oulton Broad took place in stages between 1898 and 1904. During this period a new junction was installed just to the east of the new (1901) Oulton Broad station enabling the two parallel single lines to Coke Ovens Junction to operate as a double-track section.

Brundall to Yarmouth via Acle.

In the late 1870s the Great Eastern Railway became rather concerned over the advance from the west of what was to become the Midland & Great Northern Joint Committee's line linking the East Midlands with Yarmouth. (A brief outline of this development appears in our earlier volume *Melton Constable to Yarmouth Beach*.) An answer to the perceived threat was to improve capacity eastwards from Norwich; this was achieved by securing an Act of Parliament in 1879 for a more direct line from a junction at Brundall to link up with the original 1844 line near Yarmouth. The line opened in two stages, from Yarmouth to Acle in March 1883 and from Brundall to Acle in June of the same year. The March date was no doubt seen as significant by the GER in that it "stole the thunder" of the rival line who didn't manage to open their final cross country link until the following month.

The connection shortened the distance between Norwich and Yarmouth by just over two miles and was single throughout, with a passing loop at Acle.

PASSENGER SERVICES

These routes became extremely popular as the public's desire and opportunity for seaside holidays increased. However, the services quoted in the following summary reflect the day-to-day situation experienced by the resident population to satisfy their business and domestic requirements. The number of trains in the down direction only are mentioned, it being assumed that those in the up direction were much the same. Since 1883 three separate services with varying stopping patterns have operated over these lines; it is felt that any attempt to provide comprehensive details would test the patience of the reader. The summary, therefore, paints only a very broad picture.

Norwich to Yarmouth/Lowestoft via Reedham

On the opening of the line to Yarmouth in 1844 there were four weekday services, the first leaving Norwich at 9.00am and the last at 7.00pm

When the line to Lowestoft opened in 1847, services were provided by detaching a portion at Reedham from those trains destined for Yarmouth. This arrangement continued for over one hundred years, although on some occasions connections were provided by a separate "shuttle" to and from Lowestoft.

Prior to the opening of the direct line from Brundall to Yarmouth via Acle, the March 1882 timetable listed eight trains to Yarmouth every weekday, each one also providing a service to Lowestoft from Reedham. Most called at all intermediate stations, although Cantley was served on request only and Berney Arms was limited to just three, again on request. All of them served all stations on the Lowestoft line.

By March 1920, Yarmouth was still limited to eight through trains from Norwich each day with Cantley restored to full status and the request stops at Berney Arms doubled to six. All stations on the Lowestoft line also enjoyed eight services in conjunction with those serving Yarmouth; but there were, in addition, two trains from Norwich shown as running to Lowestoft. These were both through trains from Liverpool Street, one of which ran non-stop from Norwich to Reedham, but called at all stations thence to the Suffolk resort; the other called at all stations between Norwich and Lowestoft and also detached a portion for Yarmouth at Reedham.

Following the local introduction of diesel unit workings, a Winter timetable of 1957/8 showed an astonishing improvement to 20 services to Yarmouth via this route, some of which were through trains with others provided by shuttles from Reedham to Yarmouth in connection with some of the 22 daily trains connecting Norwich and Lowestoft. Stops at the better used intermediate stations were generous, but those such as Buckenham and Somerleyton were omitted by some trains.

By 1960 the two services were totally independent, with none relying on shuttles to/from Reedham. This situation has continued into the 21st century, although from the late 1960s the number of trains serving Yarmouth by this route gradually declined to the point where only two such could be found in the 2009 timetable providing the opportunity for Cantley and Reedham residents to visit the Norfolk seaside town by a direct route. By contrast, the Lowestoft line had seen a gradual improvement from 15 trains in 1969 to 19 in 2009. Since 1988 these had generally included three services running non-stop from Norwich to Oulton Broad.

Brundall to Yarmouth via Acle

The first section of line was served by a shuttle service from Yarmouth to Acle with four weekday trains in each direction. When the line opened throughout, five weekday trains connected Norwich with Yarmouth, all calling at Brundall, Lingwood and Acle. By March 1920 the service had been increased to eight.

Post-World War II recovery in the Summer of 1946 showed eleven trains while, well into the DMU era, no less than 17 trains appeared in the 1969 timetable. Five of these were, in fact, hauled main line services returning in the evening to the servicing sidings at Yarmouth after shuttling from Norwich to Liverpool Street and back during the day.

This level has continued much the same into the 21st Century, except that, since the transfer of carriage servicing to Norwich in 1982, weekday trains are all diesel multiple units.

1. Norwich to Yarmouth
NORWICH THORPE

1. This 1957 plan at a scale of 6ins. to 1 mile depicts an area similar to that of the 1883 plan used in our earlier volume *Ely to Norwich* and enables changes that had taken place both on and off the railway to be studied. The branches that follow head off almost due east past Wensum Junction at the eastern edge.

1. The station built for the Yarmouth & Norwich Railway proved inadequate to handle the increase in rail traffic as further lines reached the city, and a new, larger terminus was opened on adjoining land in 1886, allowing the earlier station to be demoted to a goods depot. Here is the old station on 8th October 1911, with the clock tower, a feature of the original building, still standing. A goods station remained on this site until the 1980s, but bomb damage and ongoing redevelopment had removed most of the original features by the time it was eventually demolished. (GERS/Windwood Collection)

2. Class N7 0-6-0T no. 69708 stands in platform 5 with a train for Yarmouth during the early 1950s. The discs on the buffer beam indicate that it will be travelling via Acle. Trains on the Yarmouth via Acle, Yarmouth via Reedham and the Cromer lines each carried a different configuration of lamps or discs, in order to identify the route they were taking, while Lowestoft services used the standard headcode denoting the type of train. A new platform 6 was built in the area to the right of the barrows in 1955. (A.G.Forsyth/Initial Photographics)

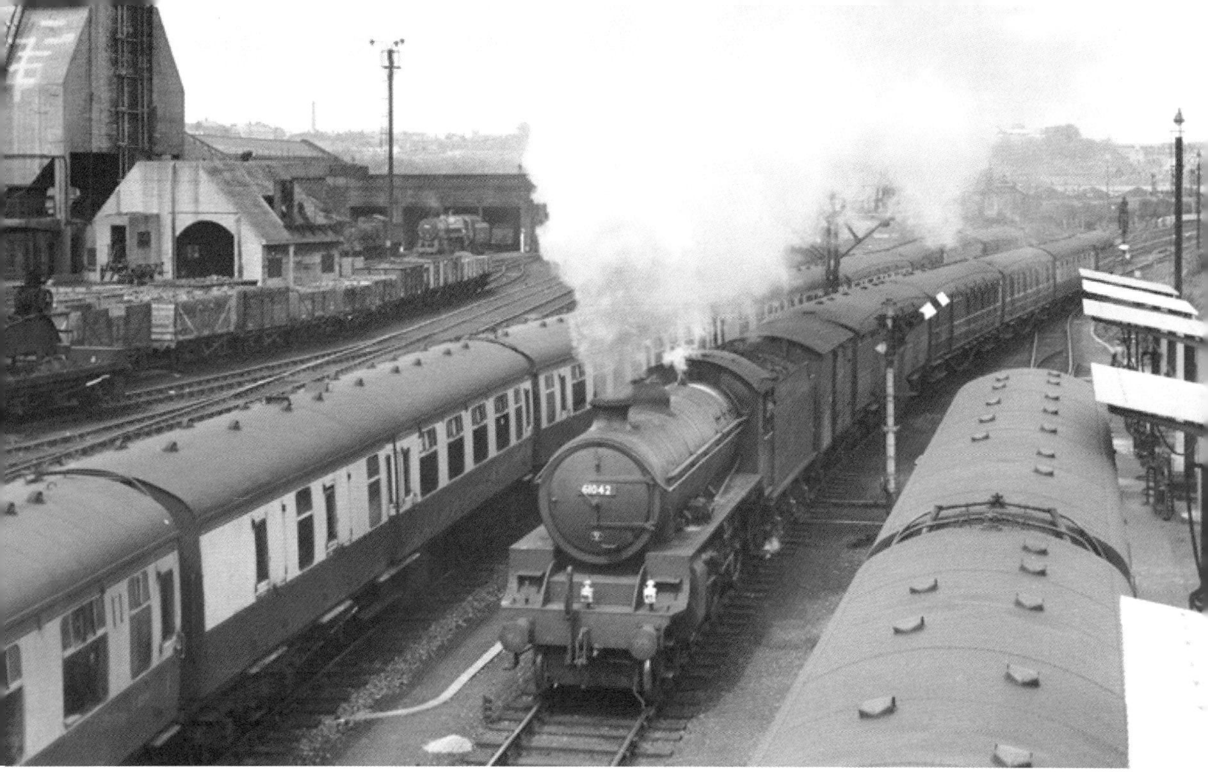
61042

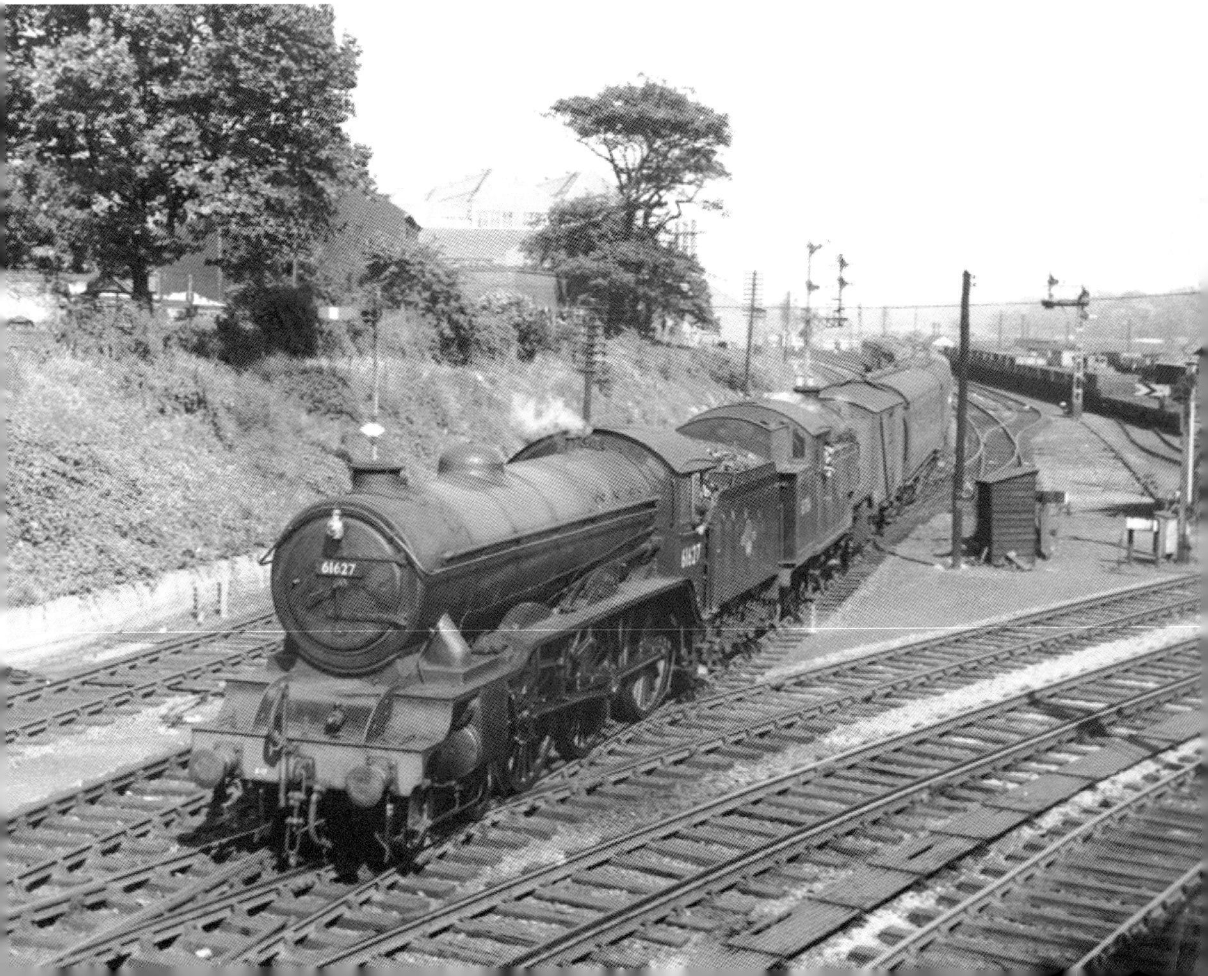
61627
61627

← 3. Class B1 4-6-0 no.61042 accelerates away from the station on Saturday 31st May 1958 with a train for Yarmouth. This engine, too, is displaying the headcode which shows it will be taking the Acle route. In the distance, a class J17 0-6-0 and a gleaming "Britannia" stand outside the locomotive shed. (B.Harrison)

← 4. Later that summer, on 19th July, Class B17/6 4-6-0 no. 61627 *Aske Hall* and class L1 2-6-4T no. 67704 approach Norwich from the coast. They are heading a train destined for Peterborough East, which will reverse in the station before continuing its journey. Part of the train had originated from Yarmouth Vauxhall at 3.40 pm, whilst the remaining coaches had left Lowestoft Central five minutes earlier. The two portions were combined at Reedham.
(M. Fordham)

5. With the destination blind showing "Yarmouth", a class 101 DMU stands in platform 5 on 5th May 1987. No. 86220 is in platform 4, with its *The Round Tabler* nameplates covered prior to a naming ceremony which was followed by one of the first electric workings, albeit for invited guests only, from the city to Liverpool Street. Diesel multiple units began to replace steam trains on local services around Norwich as early as 1955.
(R.J.Adderson)

EAST OF NORWICH THORPE

← II. In order to avoid two expensive crossings of the navigable River Yare, a "canal" (or New Cut), just over ½ mile long, was excavated to the south of the proposed line with low level bridges to provide limited access to the original river on the north side, as shown on this 1906 edition at a scale of 6ins. to 1 mile.

6. This view of bridge no.358, looking east in 1926 prior to reconstruction the following year, shows the man-made New Cut to the right. The original river heads off to the left before regaining its original course in the far distance, having passed between the railway and Thorpe St. Andrew's parish church, the spire of which is prominent. (British Rail)

Other Middleton Press albums featuring Norwich are:
Ely to Norwich
Norwich Tramways

WHITLINGHAM JUNCTION

7. This is the signalman's view of the station, looking towards Norwich on a Winter day during the GER era. The main station buildings are on the northern platform, with a waiting room on the other side. Both are constructed largely of wood. Beyond the buildings is the footbridge, which until around 1987 still carried a builders' plate stating that it had been constructed by Arrol Bros of Glasgow in 1886. (R.J.Adderson collection)

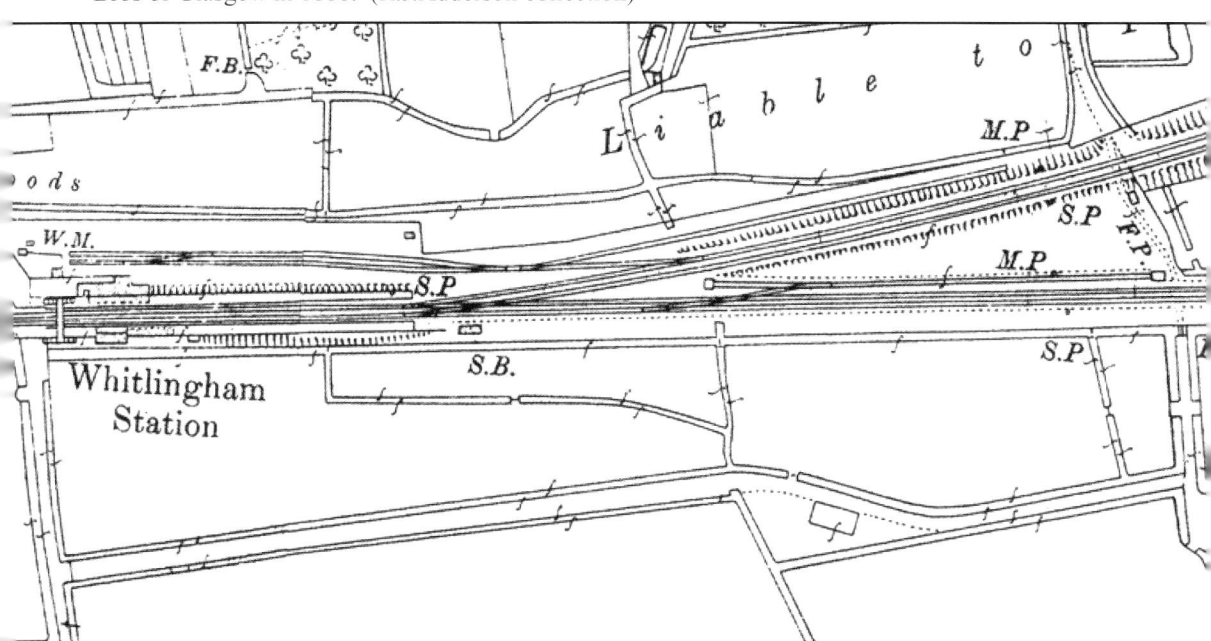

8.	A few passengers are waiting on the platform as a class D16/3 4-4-0 runs into the station with a train for Yarmouth in 1954. By now the platforms and buildings are looking somewhat tired, and the canopy has been cut away. Some coaches are stabled in the goods yard to the right: this was a regular occurrence and occasionally led to the somewhat bizarre sight of a tender-first "Britannia" arriving here with empty carriages from Norwich. (GERS/B.D.J. Walsh)

↙ III. Few alterations took place here after this 1914 plan, the main visible change being the transfer of the refuge siding shown here on the down side to the up side as seen in picture number 10. The station had been opened as an interchange facility when the first section of the line to Cromer was opened in 1874. A goods yard was not provided until 1902. Following many local protests, closure to passengers took place on 19th September 1955, at the end of the Summer timetable.

9.	A poster announces the impending closure of the station, which was first mooted in May 1954 and eventually took place some 15 months later. A census taken during June 1954 revealed a daily weekday average of 6 passengers joining and 98 leaving up trains, whilst 7 left and 92 boarded down trains. With 59 trains a day calling, this was an average of just over three passengers per train. The economics of the situation were not helped by the fact that some £7000 would need to be spent on remedial work, owing to settlement of the marshy ground, if the station were to remain open. (GERS/B.D.J.Walsh)

BRITISH RAILWAYS

WHITLINGHAM
(FOR THORPE ST. ANDREW)

WITHDRAWAL OF PASSENGER TRAIN SERVICE

The British Transport Commission hereby give notice that on and from 19th September 1955 Whitlingham station will be closed to passenger train traffic.

Passengers will be catered for at Norwich (Thorpe) station and by the omnibus services operating in the area.

Parcels traffic may be handed in at Norwich (Thorpe) station for despatch by passenger train, or may be addressed there "to be called for". A parcels collection and delivery service will be provided at the appropriate charges from Norwich (Thorpe) station.

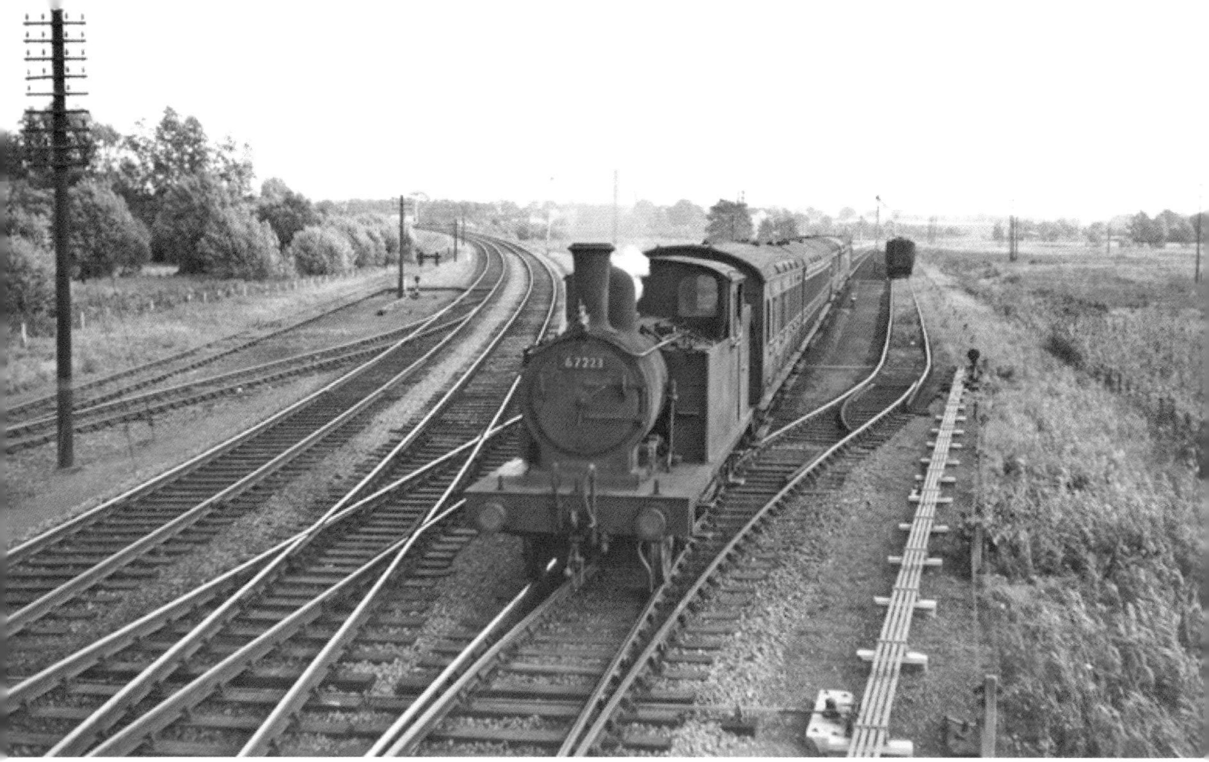

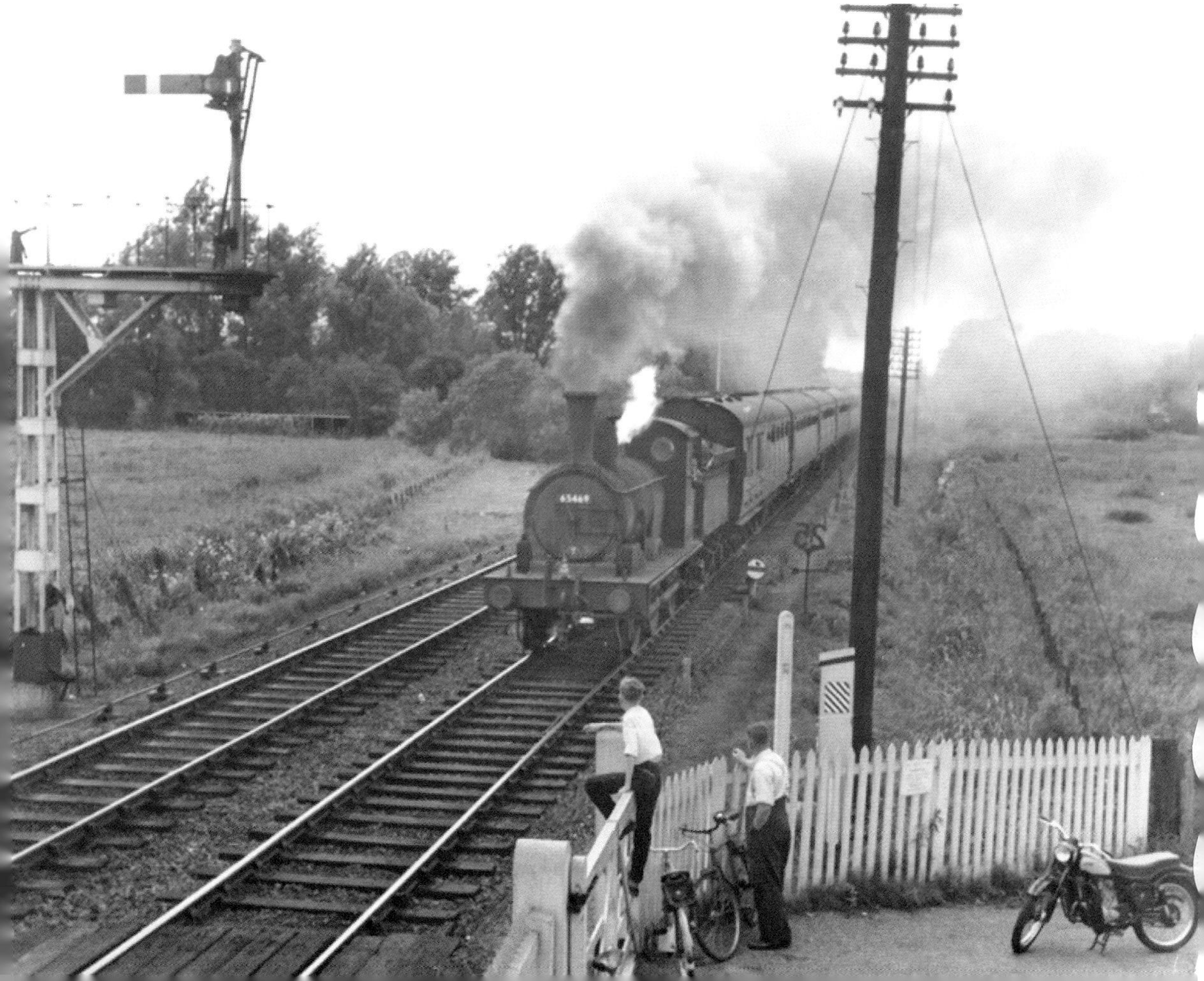

← 10. Here we have another view from the signalbox, this time looking eastwards around 1954, with the Cromer line climbing away to the left, and the line towards Brundall heading out across the marshes. Class F6 2-4-2T no.67223 is approaching with a stopping train from Lowestoft. (I.C.Allen/Transport Treasury)

← 11. After the station closed, the footbridge remained in place, giving access to the marshland south of the railway. This was a popular spot for youngsters in the 1950s, as they could fish for tiddlers on the marshes, observe the boats on the river, and watch the trains go by. On Summer Saturdays especially, there was a seemingly endless procession of these. Seen from the footbridge steps, class J15 0-6-0 no. 65469 heads a train for Yarmouth past an admiring audience in 1959. The single lamp on the buffer beam shows that it will be taking the Reedham line to the resort, while the Stanier coaches suggest that this is a holiday train which had originated in the Midlands. (M.Fordham)

12. The goods yard remained in use for general traffic, mostly coal, until July 1964. A rail-served cement depot was later established on the site and the distinctive yellow "Presflo" wagons were a familiar sight here into the 1970s. Although this traffic ceased during the decade, there was a very brief resurgence in 1986, and a line of cement wagons were in the siding on 19th June that year, as no. 31415 hurried past with empty newspaper vans. (R.J.Adderson)

BRUNDALL GARDENS HALT

IV. This station was not opened until 1st August 1924 and owes its existence to F.H.Cooper, an entrepreneur of the cinema industry. He bought an estate, which included the 76 acre Brundall Gardens, in 1917 and quickly developed it as a local tourist attraction. It was located just to the east of the station and had an access immediately outside the down side station entrance as depicted in this 1928 plan. The station remained open in 2009, serving the western end of the large, but straggling, village.

13. Here we see the newly-opened station, looking westwards on 22nd September 1924. It was built cheaply - the platform walls and edging are constructed from old sleepers, the platforms are surfaced with ash, and an old GER coach body provides shelter for waiting passengers. The footbridge is of a design reminiscent of similar structures on the M&GN.
(G.L.Kenworthy collection)

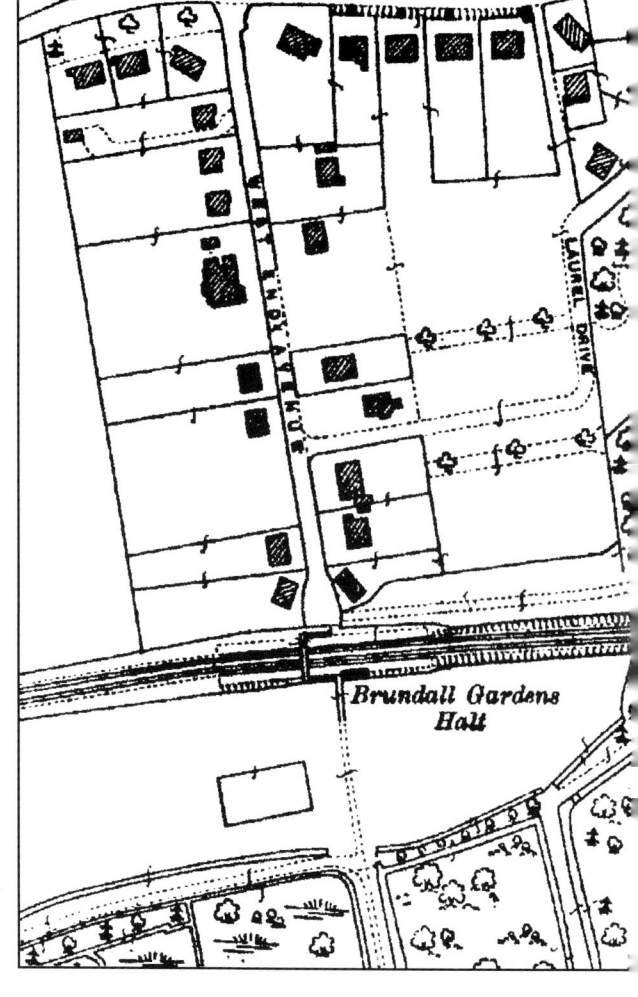

14. Now we are looking towards Brundall. It is around 1960, and little has changed since our previous picture, except that a small wooden hut has been provided on the left hand platform for staff use. The neat hedges and well-tended flower beds are noteworthy. (NRS Archive)

15. This is the scene looking in the other direction on the same day. By now, a former Great Central Railway coach body has replaced the GER example seen in picture 13. (NRS Archive)

16. During the 1970s a "bus shelter" superseded the old carriage on the up platform, and in later years further improvements were made to the platforms and lighting. All these changes are apparent on 10th August 1987, as no. 31296 heads for Lowestoft with a lightweight goods train. (J.R.Sides)

Front and back of pocket timetable.

BRITISH RAILWAYS

TRAIN SERVICES
AND
CHEAP FARES

BETWEEN
BRUNDALL
AND
NORWICH

21st September 1953
until further notice

E 542

Printed in Great Britain   C & P

DAY RETURN TICKETS
ANY DAY   ANY TRAIN
In either direction
Third class
Brundall 1/4
Brundall Gardens Halt ... 1/2
Available outward and return on day of issue only. First class day return tickets are also obtainable
Return halves of day return tickets Brundall—Norwich (Thorpe) and Brundall Gardens Halt—Norwich (Thorpe) are alternatively available between these points by Eastern Counties Omnibus Co's road services

MONTHLY SEASON TICKETS
Third class   £ s d
Brundall 1 5 9
Brundall Gardens Halt ...   1 5 0

HOLIDAY RUNABOUT
TICKETS
issued up to 31st October
on any day for one week
Unlimited travel within specified areas
For full particulars obtain pamphlet at any station
See later announcements for 1954 arrangements
The Railway Executive reserve the right to cancel or alter any of the arrangements shown herein

Published by the Railway Executive (Eastern Region)

EAST OF
BRUNDALL GARDENS HALT

17.   A GER 2-4-0 hauls a train of 6-wheel carriages along the wooded section of railway to the west of Brundall station. It is bound for Norwich, and is approaching the spot where Brundall Gardens Halt would later be built. (B.Akeroyd collection)

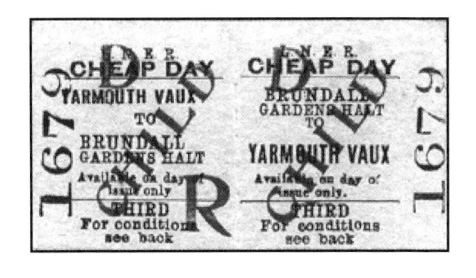

BRUNDALL

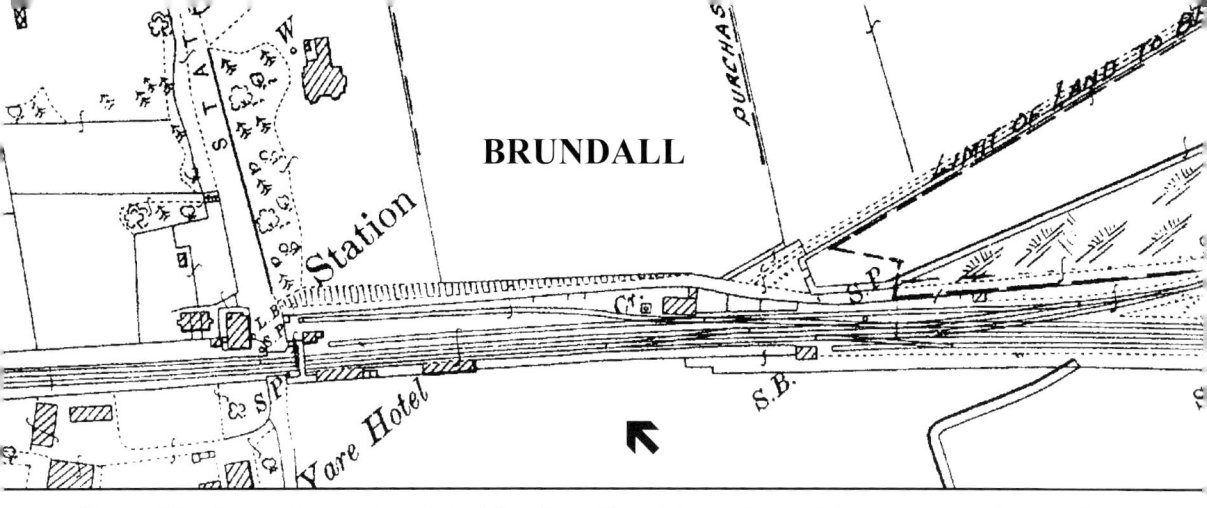

V.   The first station on the original line from Norwich was located, in common with several others, on a road which led from the village to a ferry. This was a foot ferry at Coldham Hall and it provided relatively easy access for rail passengers to and from the south side of the River Yare. The station was actually situated in the parish of Braydeston, but took the name of its larger neighbour. The basic goods facilities, consisting of two sidings, a small goods shed and a 2-ton crane are shown on the 1907 plan.

18.   Looking south along Station Road in Great Eastern days, we see the station building on the right and the gated entrance to the goods yard to the left. On the far side of the railway, a winding lane heads out through the fields towards the north bank of the River Yare. Advertisements for the London Provincial Furnishing Co of Norwich, and the Yare Hotel's Steward & Patteson Ales compete for attention, whilst halfway up the signal ladder, a young railway employee makes certain he is not left out of the picture. Little had changed in 2009, with the footbridge, crossing gates and station building all very much as they were a century earlier. However, the lane beyond the crossing had become a busy road serving the boatyards which had developed over the years. (D.Brinded collection)

19.   Members of the station staff again find themselves in the picture as a class Y14 0-6-0 arrives from Norwich with a short train of six-wheel coaches during the years before World War 1. (G.Gosling collection)

20.   The station occupied a narrow strip of land, necessitating staggered platforms. We are looking north-west along the up platform on 4th October 1911, with the station building and down platform in the distance. The covered coal shed is an interesting feature, whilst the nearby yard crane was still there in the late 1950s. Goods facilities were withdrawn in July 1964, and in 2009 the station car park occupied the area. (GERS/Windwood Collection)

21. A double-headed train stands in the station during the early 1950s. Class K1 2-6-0 no. 62017 and an unidentified class B1 4-6-0 are hauling two vans and seven coaches of varying profile, and will be taking the Acle line at the junction. (B.Reading)

→ 22. We are looking north along Station Road on 12th November 1966. The railway cottages to the left of the main station building dated back to the early days of the line and were demolished shortly after this picture was taken. (Railway Record of the British Isles/G.L.Pring)

→ 23. The junction is immediately to the east of the station. A class 101 DMU is curving away on the Acle line on 29th August 1981, whilst the double track to Reedham goes straight on in a south-easterly direction. The line from the goods yard trails in from the left, and the up siding disappears behind the signal box. (R.Powell)

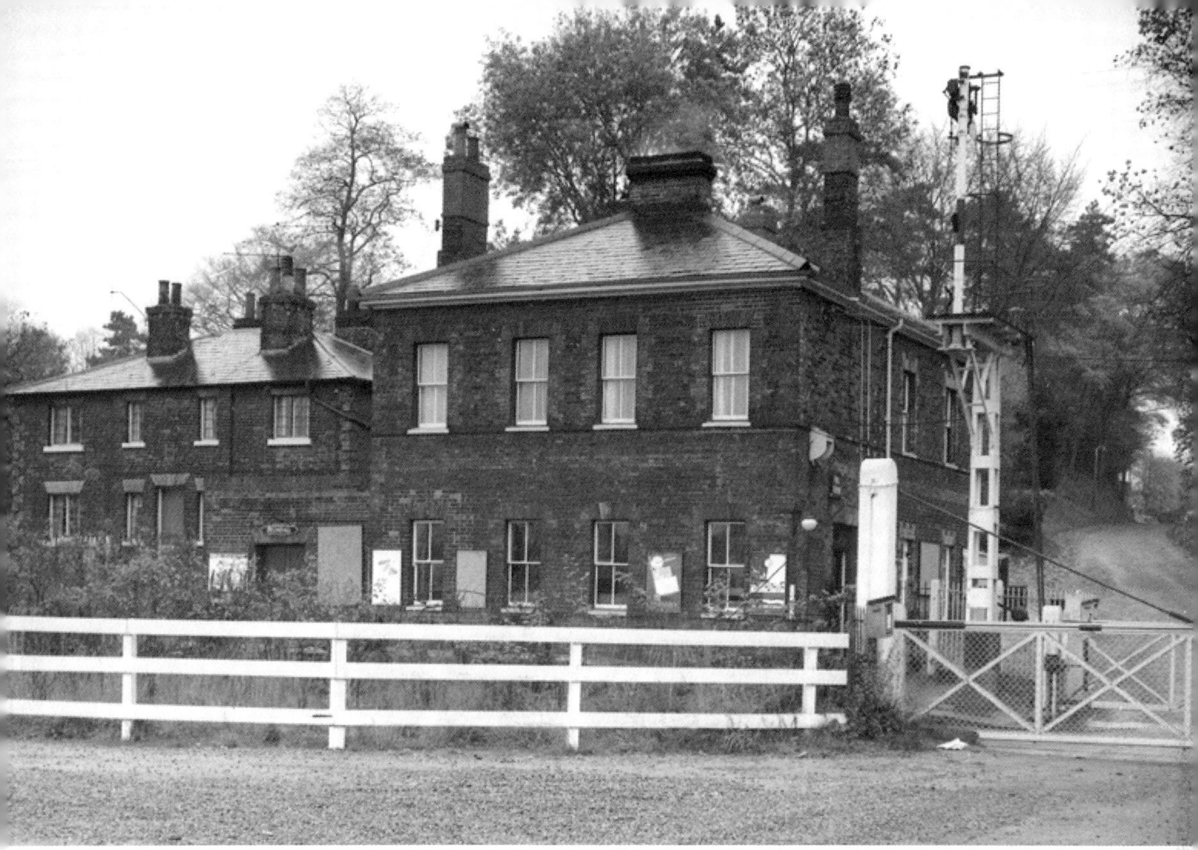

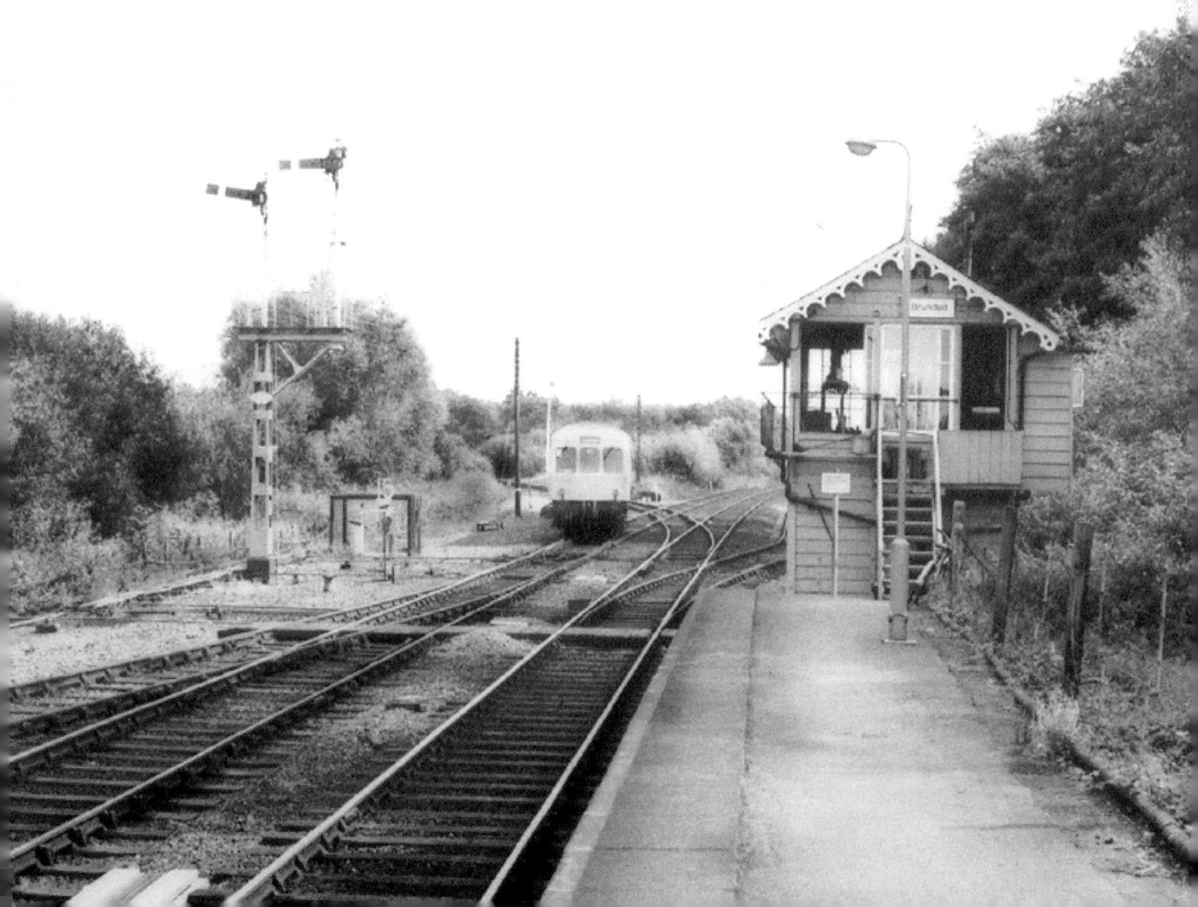

BUCKENHAM

24. The platform at this somewhat remote location is showing signs of neglect in this picture looking towards Norwich. It is around 1960, and the up starter signal is still a tall GER specimen. The station's traffic potential was limited - in 1891 Buckenham itself had a population of 95, while neighbouring Hassingham could boast just 122 residents. (NRS Archive)

VI. Without the presence of the ferry to the south, which was present by the start of the 19th century (if not earlier), it is unlikely that the hamlet, after which the station was named, would have justified the provision of a station. The 1907 plan shows its isolated location and minimal goods facilities.

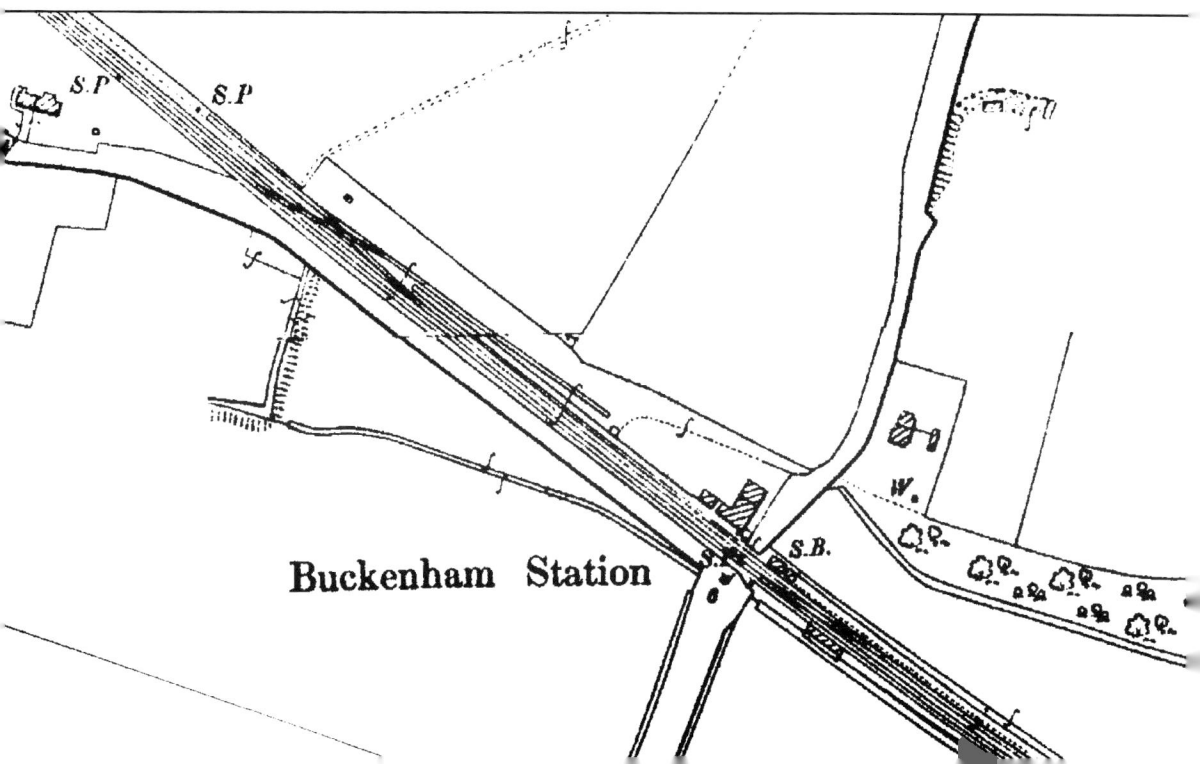

25. Now we are looking south-eastwards, with the meadows stretching away towards the distant river, as a Brush type 2 diesel heads an up passenger train on 29th August 1971. By this time, the crossover had been lifted and the Great Eastern signal had been removed. The goods facilities, never heavily used, had been withdrawn in July 1964.
(Railway Record of the British Isles/G.L.Pring)

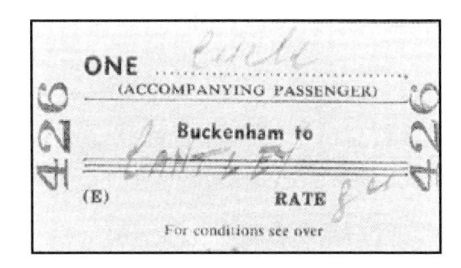

26.   No 31205 passes the station with a Summer Saturday train from Chesterfield to Yarmouth on 16th August 1980. The signal box had been reduced to the status of a ground frame in 1973, and it was taken out of use and demolished in the mid-1980s. By contrast, the station building was still standing and undergoing refurbishment in 2009. (R.J.Adderson)

27.   The number of trains stopping here declined gradually over the years. In 2009 no trains were booked to call on Mondays to Fridays, and just one train in each direction stopped on Saturdays if requested. Remarkably the service increased to a total of nine trains on Sundays in the hope of attracting visitors to nearby bird reserves. Reflecting this, the station nameboard features the logos of the Wherry Lines and the Royal Society for the Protection of Birds. (R.J.Adderson)

CANTLEY

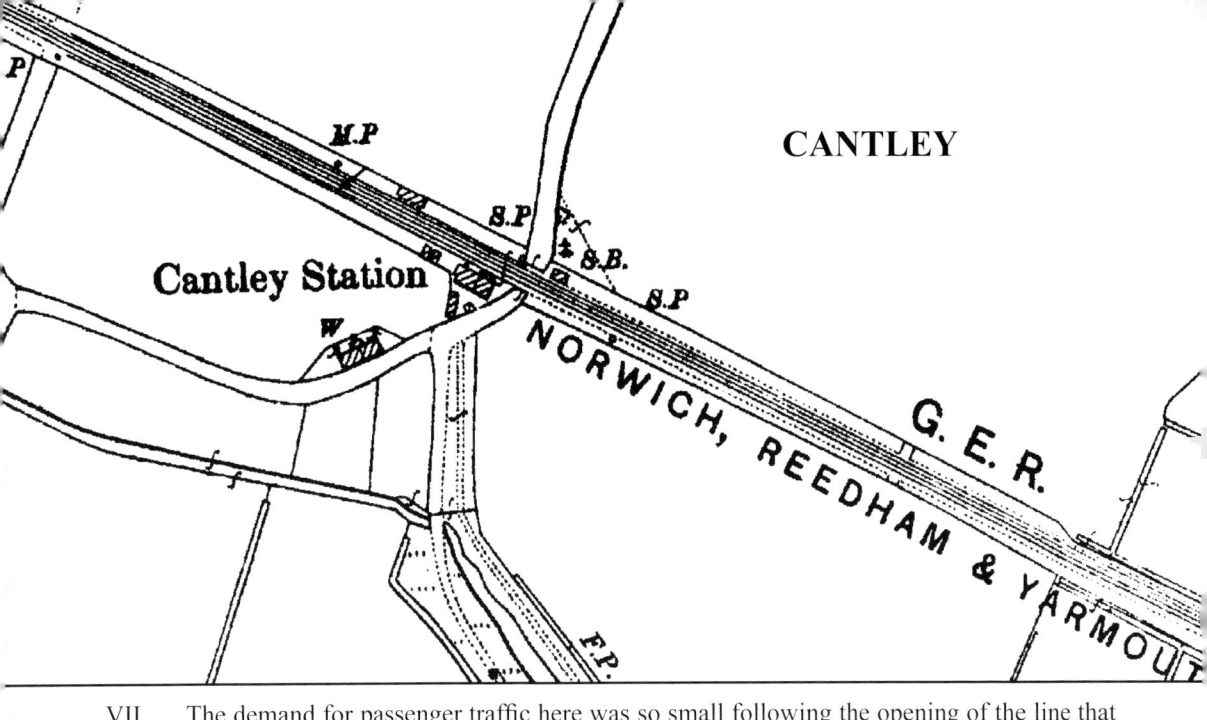

VII. The demand for passenger traffic here was so small following the opening of the line that a period of closure existed from the Autumn of 1847 until early in 1851. No goods facilities in the form of a goods yard were ever provided. This 1907 plan pre-dates the building of the sugar beet factory to the south-east of the station.

28. The silos of the sugar beet factory dominate the station as no. 31426 approaches with a Summer Saturday train from Yarmouth on 21st September 1985. Although disused since the station became unstaffed in 1965, the station building is still standing to the right of the level crossing. A step down from platform level testified to the fact that the building dated from the earliest days of the line, before raised platforms were provided. The building was demolished a few years after this picture was taken. (R.J.Adderson)

29. Traditional semaphore signals remained a feature of the Wherry Lines in 2009. A notable example was this home signal, just to the west of the platforms, with two co-acting arms owing to limited visibility for drivers of trains approaching round the curve. By this time, such signals were very rare specimens. No. 47501 *Craftsman* approaches with a train from Liverpool Street to Yarmouth on 13th June 2009. (R.J.Adderson)

30. Much of the old atmosphere survives here as a train heads away towards the coast on 15th August 2009. With the generally tidy appearance, colourful gardens, platform buildings, signalling and level crossing gates this could almost be a scene from the preservation world. A team of local volunteers, known as the Friends of Cantley station, has taken on the responsibility for looking after the station. (R.J.Adderson)

EAST OF CANTLEY

VIII. The first sugar beet factory in the country was established here in 1912 by the Anglo-Netherlands Sugar Beet Corporation. The private sidings, worked by the firm's locomotives, dealt with the incoming beet, coal, coke and limestone and were extended from time to time. By the late 1980s railborne traffic had ceased, but the factory expanded and, unlike several others in the Eastern Counties, was still operating well into the 21st century.

31. Former North Eastern Railway class H2 (later LNER class J79) 0-6-0T no.1662 was one of a succession of locomotives which worked at the factory. It operated here for some 20 years from 1937, and is seen with a typically industrial background.
(NRS Archive)

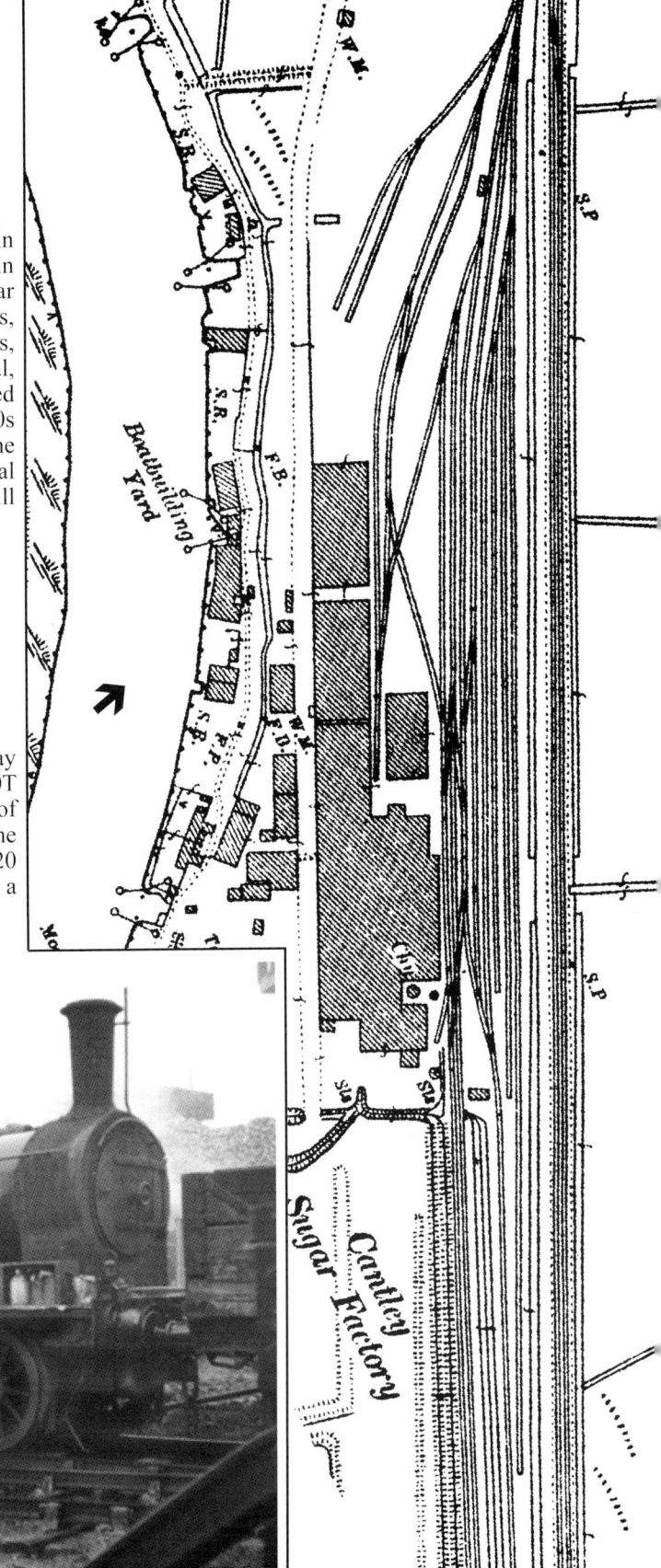

32. Hunslet 0-6-0ST *Grosvenor* was a contemporary of no.1662, serving here from 1935 until it was scrapped on site in 1958. This picture is dated 21st July 1957, at a time when rail traffic still played a major role in the operations at the factory. In 1959 7,274 railway wagons delivered 74,914 tons of sugar beet, some 16% of the total beet received. During the same year, the factory dispatched 15,771 tons of dried beet pulp and 12,770 tons of wet and pressed pulp by rail. In each case this tonnage represented some 40% of the total production. (N. Nicolson/Transport Treasury)

33. A number of internal user wagons, painted in a light green "British Sugar Corporation" livery, were a feature of the factory for many years. Some were former GER box vans, others were hopper wagons as shown here standing in a siding on 9th March 1977. The connection to the main line is on the right and the station signal box can be seen in the distance. (C.Fisher)

34. Now we have a general view inside the factory precincts on 11th June 1980, featuring one of the two Ruston & Hornsby diesel locomotives which replaced the steam engines. These operated here until rail traffic ceased around 1989. (R.Darsley)

On January 19th last, a meeting was held at the Agricultural Hall, Norwich, which showed that the opening up of the industry in Norfolk was well on its way. That the Great Eastern Railway Company are alive to the importance of the matter from their point of view is evidenced by the fact that Sir Ailwyn Fellowes, K.C.V.O., deputy Chairman of the Company presided. Amongst other influential people present were: The Earl of Leicester (Lord Lieutenant of Norfolk), Lord Hastings, Mr. G. L. Courthope, M.P. (President of the Sugar Beet Council), Sir Rider Haggard, Mr. H. H. Boyle, M.P., and the meeting, which was summoned by the Norfolk Chamber of Agriculture was well attended by a number of the leading farmers of the county.

From "Great Eastern Railway Magazine"
May 1912.

35. The photographer leans out of a passing train on 29th March 1986 to record the connection into the factory complex. Although the turnout remained in 2009, the tracks within the factory had long been lifted, and trains carrying limestone for use at the factory were forced to transfer their load into lorries at Norwich. (R.Powell)

IX. Further east, there was an attempt after World War I to develop a chilled meat factory by a firm known as Imchillco. Although siding connections controlled by Cantley East signal box, shown on this 1928 edition at 20 ins to 1 mile, were installed at a cost to the GER of around £4000, poor structural design of the factory caused problems and the factory was abandoned before production started.

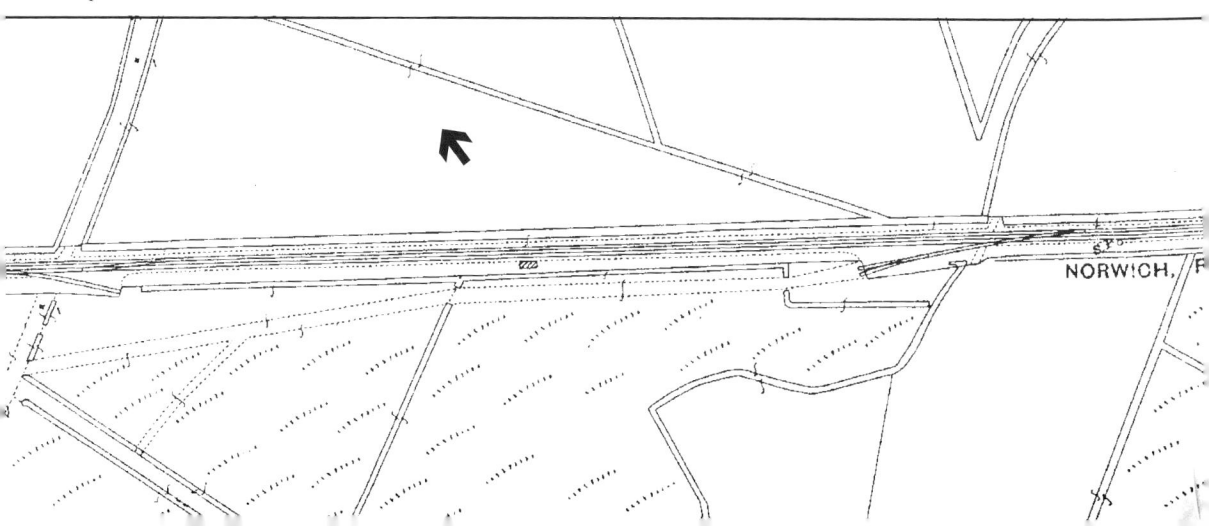

REEDHAM

36. Seen from the eastern end of the up platform, a GER 2-4-0 has drawn forward from a lengthy goods train in order to take water. This picture dates from around 1880, and clearly shows the island platform which was abolished when the trackwork was modified in connection with the doubling of the line to Lowestoft. (Norfolk County Council Library and Information service)

37. Now we are looking towards Norwich on 26th September 1911, with passengers waiting on the platform, while two members of the station staff hold a conversation at track level. A selection of crates and other merchandise await transhipment on the loading dock and a cattle wagon is standing in the siding. (GERS/Windwood Collection)

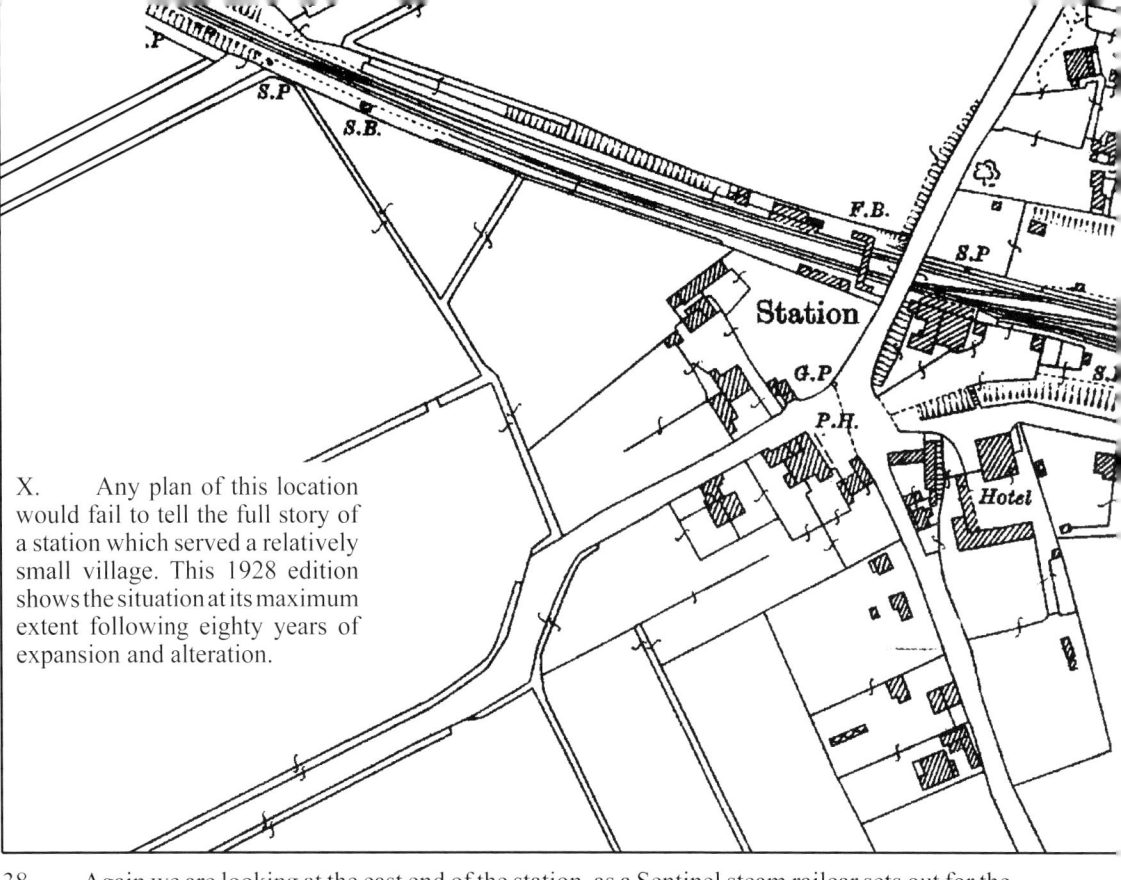

X. Any plan of this location would fail to tell the full story of a station which served a relatively small village. This 1928 edition shows the situation at its maximum extent following eighty years of expansion and alteration.

38. Again we are looking at the east end of the station, as a Sentinel steam railcar sets out for the coast during the 1920s. The three-storey Station Master's house is prominent in the centre of the picture – the top storey had been added to the original building in 1893. To the left of this are the cattle pens. These are remarkably close to the passenger platform, and at times must have provided interesting aromas for waiting passengers to savour. (J.Hull collection)

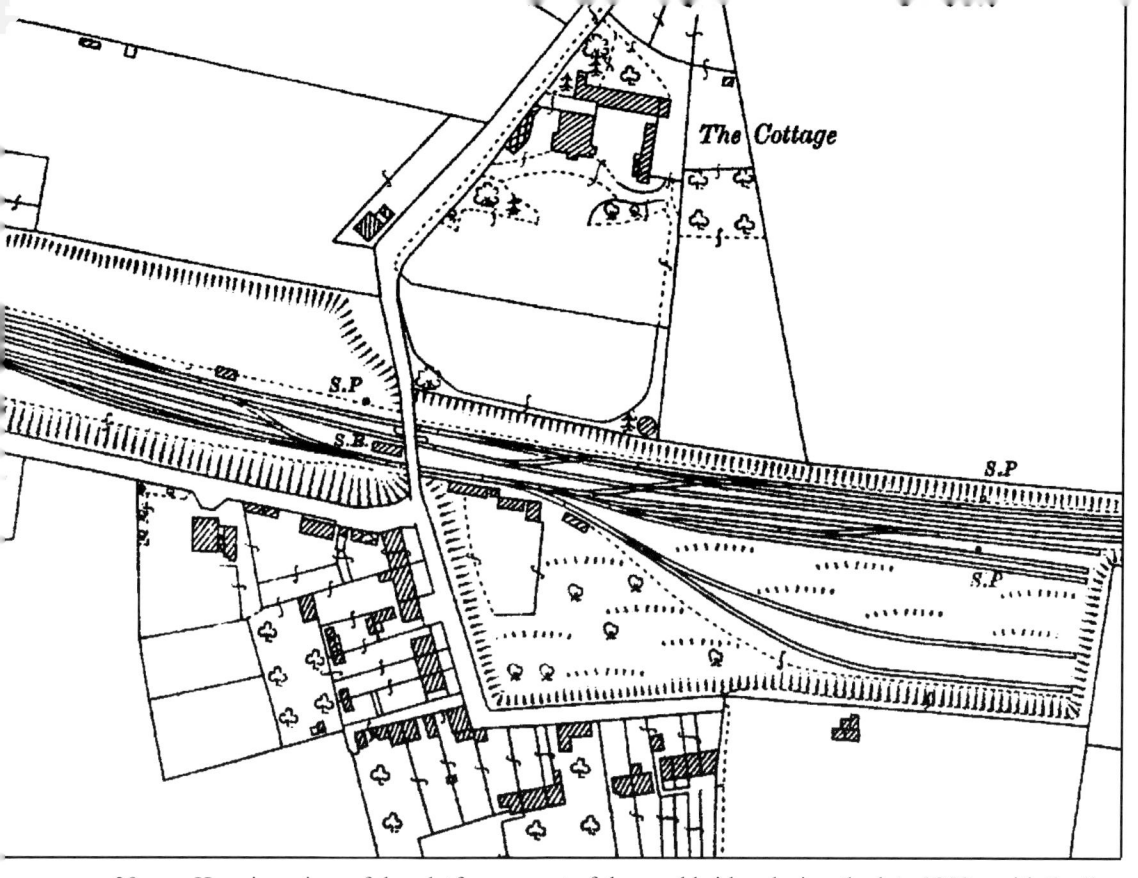

39.   Here is a view of the platforms west of the road bridge during the late 1950s, with the line beyond curving away towards Cantley. Fifty years later the waiting shelter on the down platform was still standing, complete with awning, but by then the water tower was a very distant memory. The space between the tracks through the station was once occupied by the island platform shown in picture 36. (NRS Archive)

40. Seen from the road bridge east of the station, no. D8202 heads for the coast in August 1960. Its train is made up of a modern BR Mark 1 vehicle, an LNER-built articulated twin set and four varied non-corridor coaches. At first, dieselisation did not bring standardisation. (W.J.Naunton)

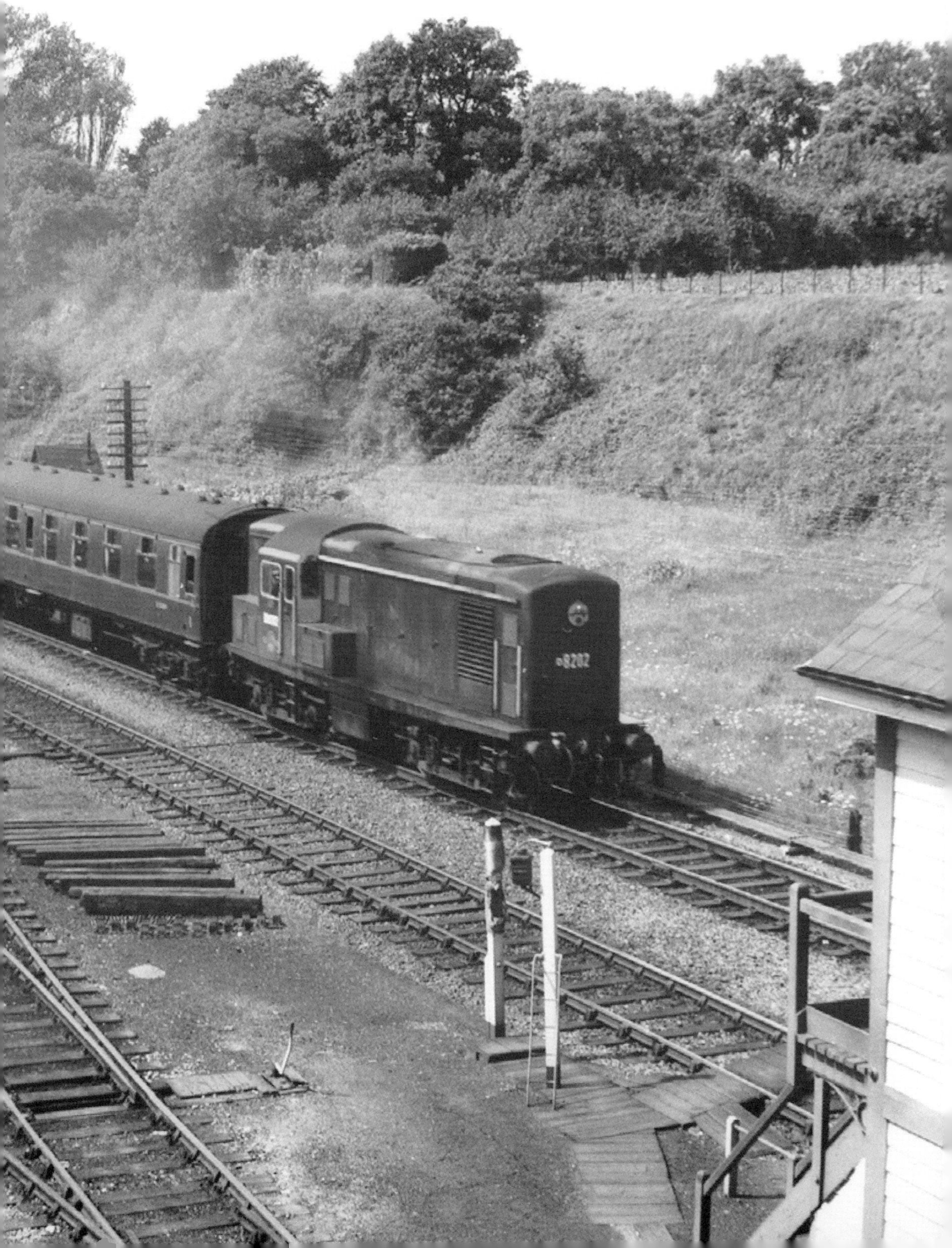
D8202

41. Looking eastwards from the same bridge, we see a class K3 2-6-0 approaching the station with a train from Yarmouth, again in August 1960. The engine is carrying an express passenger headcode, but the mixture of Stanier and Gresley coaches provides no clue to its destination. (W.J.Naunton)

42. A class 156 sets out from the station in June 2009, with the signal showing that it will be taking the line to Yarmouth. The track layout has been reduced over the years but the loading dock seen in picture 37 is still there beyond the platform ramp. Another reminder of bygone days is the siding ending in buffer stops to the left of the train. This was formerly used by engines waiting between duties, in the days when trains were divided and joined here. (R.J.Adderson)

EAST OF REEDHAM

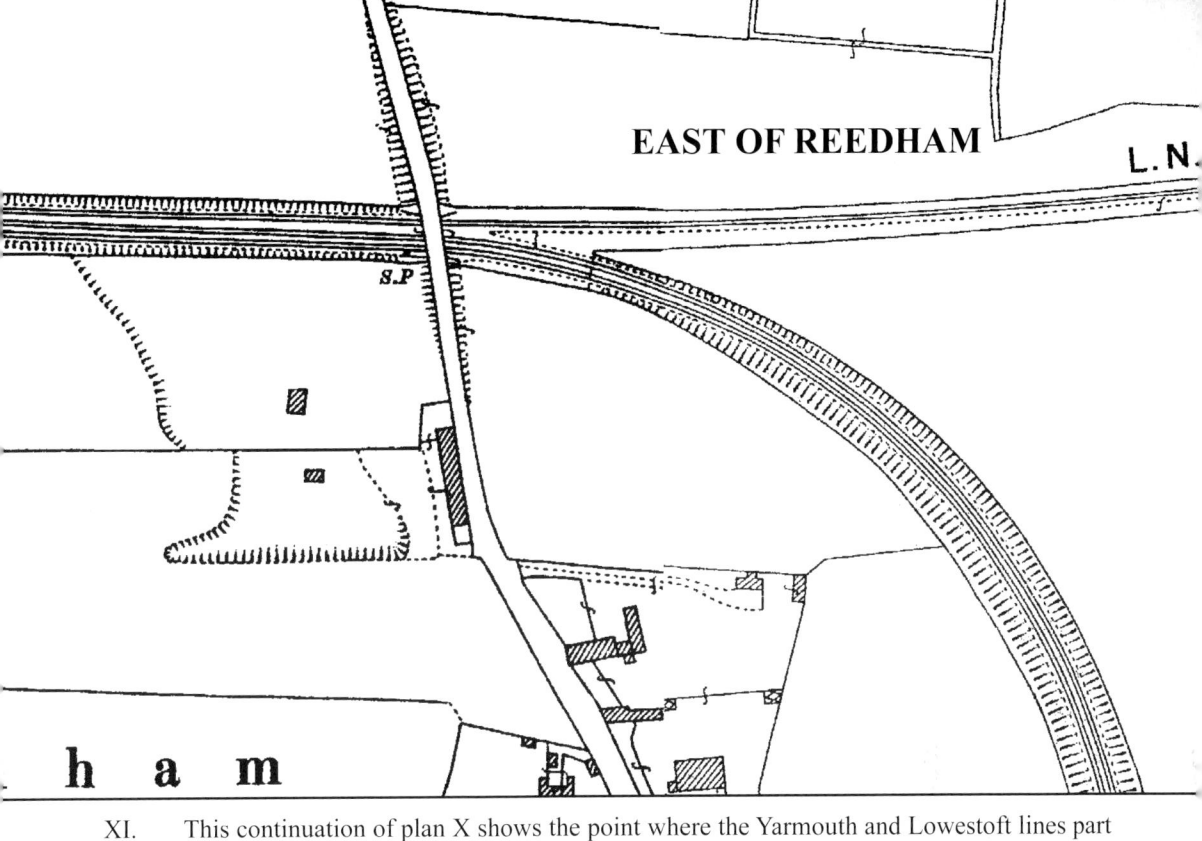

S.P

L.N.

h a m

XI. This continuation of plan X shows the point where the Yarmouth and Lowestoft lines part company half a mile or so to the east of the station.

43. Class D16/3 4-4-0 no. 62555 takes the single track towards Yarmouth while the double-track line to Lowestoft curves sharply away to the south-east underneath the bridge.
(I.C.Allen/Transport Treasury)

BERNEY ARMS

44. This little community could be reached by rail and river, but had no road access other than this muddy track, winding across the marshes from the nearest road some three miles away. We are looking south-eastwards, with the pub and the river half a mile away beyond the gates. This picture, and the next three, all date from 19th November 1966. (Railway Record of the British Isles/G.L.Pring)

45. The building to the east of the railway served a variety of functions. As shown by the sign on the wall, part of it acted as a Post Office, which was reached through the door in the porch to the right. The centre portion was the waiting room and ticket office, while the remainder was residential. Above the door, a wooden casing protects the bell that was rung to advise waiting passengers that their train had left either Yarmouth or Reedham. The structure was demolished around 1970. (Railway Record of the British Isles/G.L.Pring)

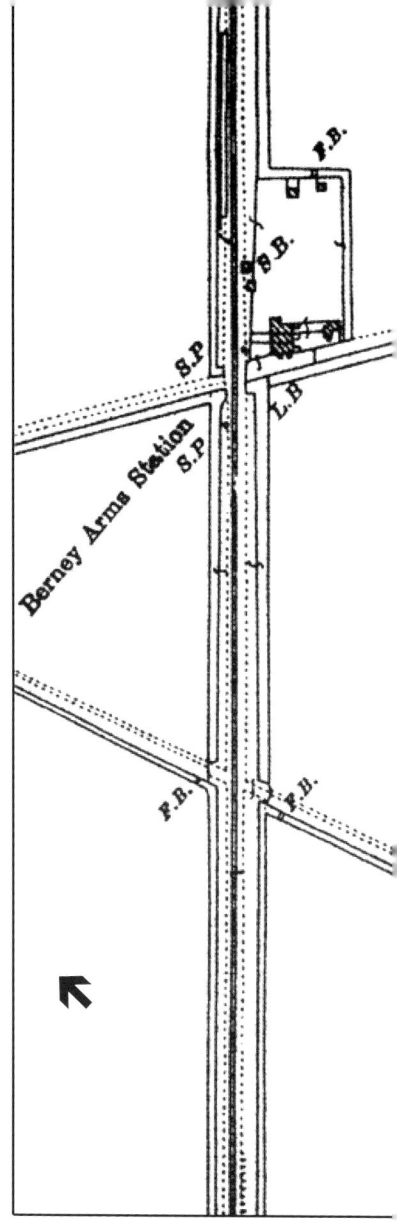

XII. The station is named after the nearby inn on the north bank of the River Yare. The inn, which probably dates from the eighteenth century, was in turn named after the Berney family who owned much of the surrounding land. It was at their insistence that the station was provided and, in 2009, it remains one of the most inaccessible in the country. The plan dates from 1928.

46. Wooden planking running from the level crossing up on to the platform provided a solid surface for carts, prams and indeed pedestrians. Without it, an iron-wheeled barrow laden with milk churns, for example, would soon have become stuck. The facilities were undoubtedly basic, but the station was the hub of the scattered community in many ways. A former resident recalls that he was one of some 14 children who travelled daily by train to school in Reedham in the late 1940s, while his grandmother's coffin was also taken away by train. As well as groceries and newspapers, the post arrived by rail, and as late as September 1983 a local newspaper article featured the postman who travelled from Yarmouth by train to deliver mail in the area. The signalbox was abolished shortly after these pictures were taken, and was moved a short distance to become a beer store at the nearby pub, before being returned to a railway environment at Mangapps Farm Museum in the late 1980s. (Railway Record of the British Isles/ G.L.Pring)

47. The short platform was open to the elements, with a nameboard, a few oil lamps, and a rather rickety-looking seat for any waiting passengers. Beyond the platform end, the line stretches away into the distance, heading dead straight across the marshes towards Yarmouth. (Railway Record of the British Isles/G.L.Pring)

48. In 2009 the station catered almost exclusively for leisure activities. Just four trains called on weekdays, but no less than five in each direction were timetabled to stop on Sundays, allowing visitors to enjoy the solitude of the area. The platform had been cut back to one coach length many years earlier, but it is good to note that a replacement nameboard, in traditional style, had been installed in 2003. A somewhat insubstantial waiting shelter of very limited capacity was erected at the same time. No 47832 approaches with one of the Saturday Only trains from Yarmouth to Liverpool Street on 1st August 2009. (R.J.Adderson)

BREYDON JUNCTION

XIII. This junction, together with its signal box, was provided in 1883 when the first section of the new line from Brundall was opened. It is shown on this plan of 1928 and there was little, if any, change until the junction was simplified and the signal box closed in 1977.

49. Some seven miles from both Acle and Reedham, the two lines converged at this remote spot for the last mile or so into Yarmouth. A train passes the lonely signal box as it heads onto the Acle line on 3rd August 1969. The box was closed in November 1977, when the junction was abolished, and since then the two routes have run as separate single lines into Yarmouth.
(Railway Record of the British Isles/G.L.Pring)

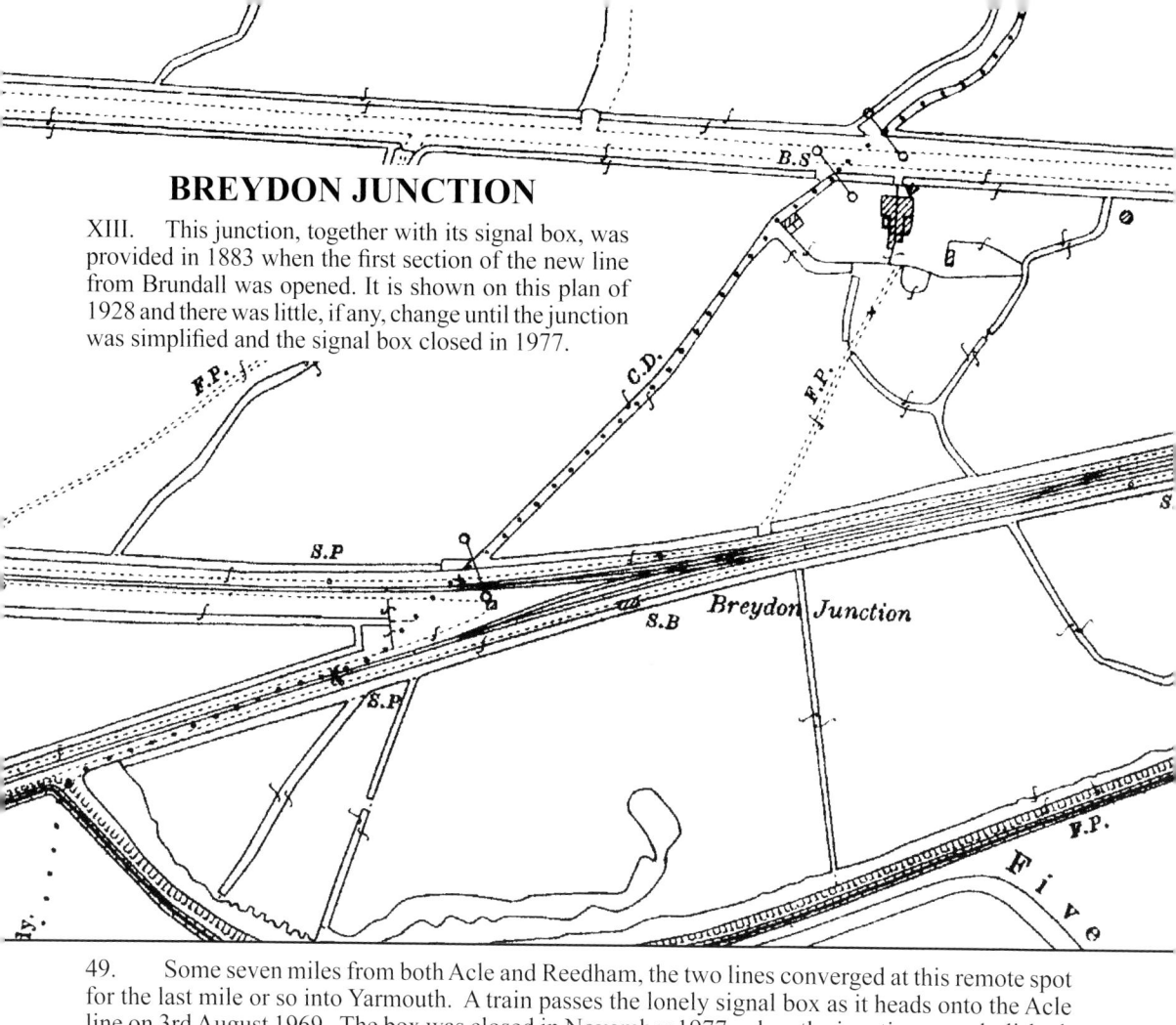

YARMOUTH VAUXHALL

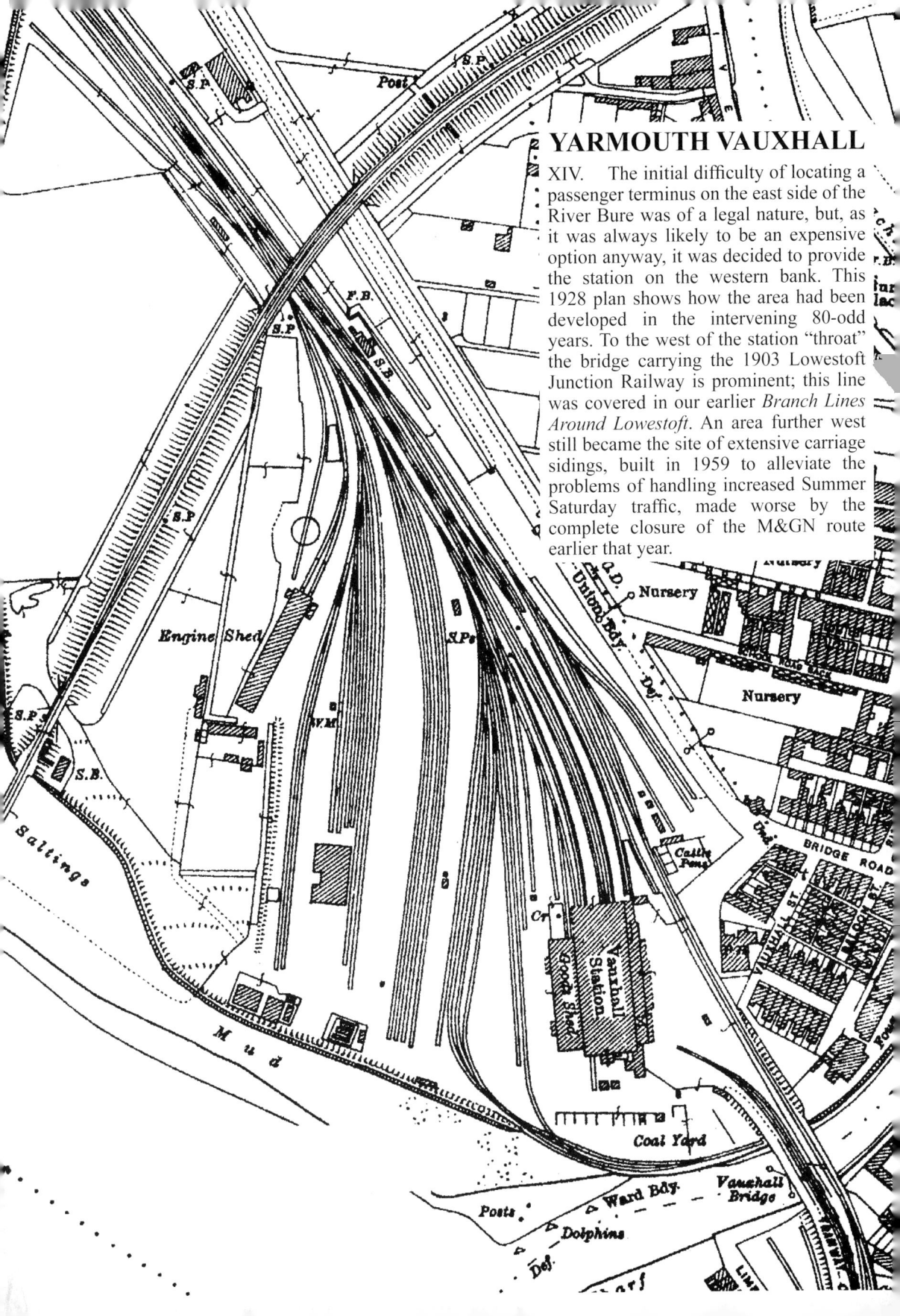

XIV. The initial difficulty of locating a passenger terminus on the east side of the River Bure was of a legal nature, but, as it was always likely to be an expensive option anyway, it was decided to provide the station on the western bank. This 1928 plan shows how the area had been developed in the intervening 80-odd years. To the west of the station "throat" the bridge carrying the 1903 Lowestoft Junction Railway is prominent; this line was covered in our earlier *Branch Lines Around Lowestoft*. An area further west still became the site of extensive carriage sidings, built in 1959 to alleviate the problems of handling increased Summer Saturday traffic, made worse by the complete closure of the M&GN route earlier that year.

50. This is the busy scene looking south-eastwards towards the terminus on 26th September 1911. The two island platforms of the passenger station are to the left and the amount of goods traffic in the extensive yard emphasises the commercial importance of the town at that time. This was one of three railway termini in the town, each with their own share of the traffic on offer. (GERS/Windwood Collection)

51. We are now looking in the opposite direction from a similar viewpoint on the same day. Two locomotives stand adjacent to the well-stocked coaling platform, and the locomotive shed is out of the picture to the left. The bridge beyond the signalbox carries the M&GN line from Yarmouth Beach to North Gorleston Junction and ultimately Lowestoft. (GERS/Windwood Collection)

52. Class J15 0-6-0 no. 7566 stands at the platform with the 5.30 pm train to Norwich via Acle on Sunday 29th April 1934. The station would remain gas lit until it was extensively modernised in 1959. (H.F.Wheeler collection per R.S.Carpenter)

53. The driver looks back along the train as class D16/3 4-4-0 no. 2524 backs the empty coaches for a Norwich local into the station. Beyond the train is the bridge carrying the M&GN line, while the large building on the left was demolished when new carriage sidings were installed in 1959. The picture dates from the early days of British Railways, although the engine still carries its LNER number on the buffer beam. (B.Reading)

54. Class D16/3 4-4-0 no 62613 stands outside the engine shed during the 1950s, while a sister engine is half-hidden inside. Although the shed lost its allocation of locomotives in 1959, the building remained standing into the 1980s. (R.S.Carpenter)

➔ 55. In terms of passenger usage, the station was at its busiest on Summer Saturdays during the 1950s and early 1960s. Looking forward to long sunny days on the beach, expectant holidaymakers emerge from a train from the Midlands on one such day in 1953. (Archant Norwich)

From the 1913 "Official Guide to the Great Eastern Railway"

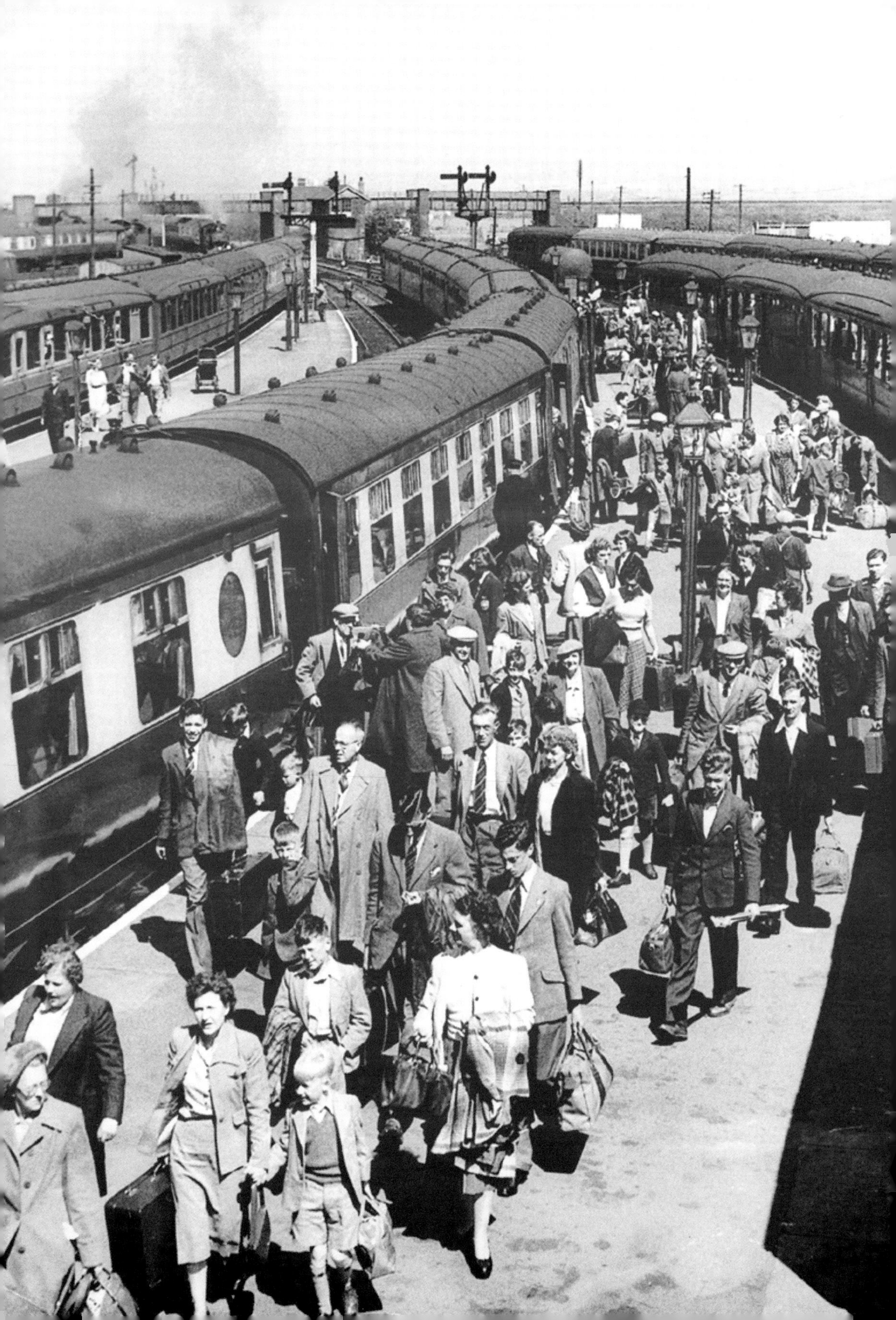

56. The closure of the M&GN line in February 1959 meant that much of the holiday traffic previously handled at Beach station was diverted here. Various improvements, including carriage sidings and platform extensions, were made in order to deal with this extra traffic. Work was not complete on 18th July 1959, when only one of the island platforms had been lengthened. A class K3 2-6-0 stands by the water crane to the left, and behind it the embankment of the M&GN line has been removed to provide infill for the new carriage sidings, although the bridge still spans the station approach. Observers noted a total of 31 long-distance trains arriving and departing between 9 am and 5.15 pm that day, handled by a variety of locomotives – 12 K3 2-6-0s, three 4MT 2-6-0s, six Brush Type 2 diesels and one each of classes J15 0-6-0, B1 4-6-0 and "Britannia" 4-6-2. During this time, some 34 local workings were also timetabled in and out of the station. The signalmen must have been very busy people indeed. (A.W.E. Hoskins)

57. The line to the docks ran out past the cattle pens and over a level crossing spanning the station approach road, which was for a time also the main road into the town. In this 1959 photograph an old coach body in the foreground contrasts with the modern goods office beyond. There is photographic evidence that passengers were on occasion forced to board their train from the cattle dock, but we do not know whether this was just an isolated instance or a regular occurrence at busy times. (G. L Kenworthy collection)

58. The frontage of the station was modified in contemporary style as part of the 1959 improvement scheme. Here is an animated scene from the time when it was new, with a policeman keeping a close eye on the proceedings. (GERS/B.D.J.Walsh)

59. In later years, the 1959 carriage sidings provided a servicing area for the coaches used on the Norwich to London services, and despite limited facilities and lack of shelter this continued until 1982. Since then they have been increasingly neglected, seeing only occasional use for freight traffic or loco stabling. Here we see a diesel shunter at work in the sidings during the early 1980s. (G.L.Kenworthy)

60. The goods yard continued to handle an occasional wagon load of coal into 1984, but the whole area was transformed over the next few years. A bypass road was built on the M&GN alignment, bridging the station approach, and the goods yard area was swallowed up by a supermarket. No. 31135 sets out with the 10.45 train for Birmingham on 29th July 1989, while a sister engine waits to follow with another Summer Saturday train, the 11.08 for Liverpool Street. The photographer is standing on the new road bridge, and the station is somewhat hemmed in between the supermarket and a dual carriageway. It is a striking contrast with the acres of railway land we saw from a similar viewpoint in picture 50. (J.R.Sides)

61. With changing social and travel patterns, long distance Summer Saturday traffic declined during the later years of the 20th century, and in 2007 consisted of just two through trains in each direction between Liverpool Street and the resort. These were notable in that the electric locomotive remained coupled to the train, which was diesel-hauled to and from Norwich. No. 90002 stands at the buffers on 11th August 2007, some 19 miles from the nearest electrified line. (R.J.Adderson)

2. Yarmouth Tramway

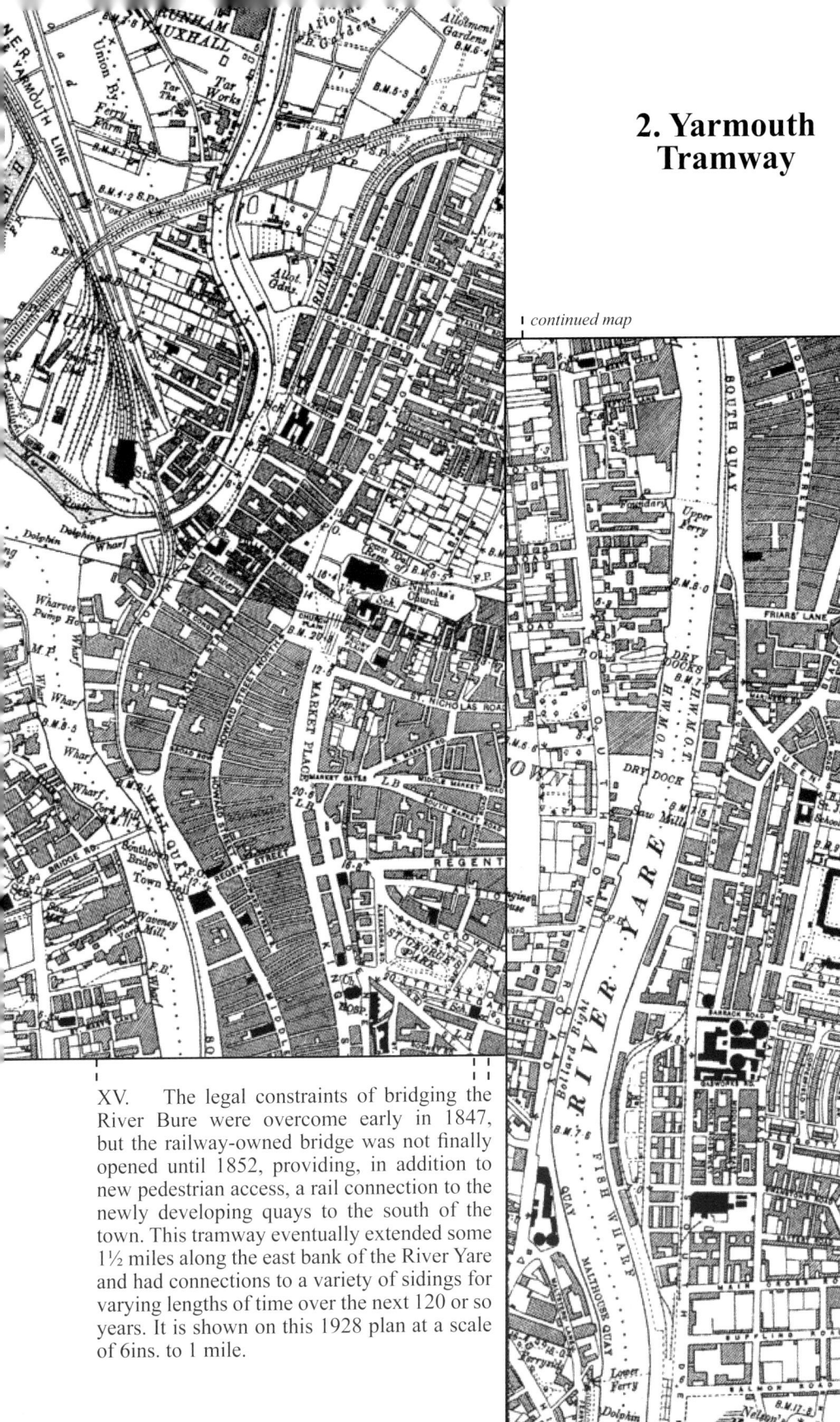

XV. The legal constraints of bridging the River Bure were overcome early in 1847, but the railway-owned bridge was not finally opened until 1852, providing, in addition to new pedestrian access, a rail connection to the newly developing quays to the south of the town. This tramway eventually extended some 1½ miles along the east bank of the River Yare and had connections to a variety of sidings for varying lengths of time over the next 120 or so years. It is shown on this 1928 plan at a scale of 6ins. to 1 mile.

62. Returning from the quayside, a diesel shunter heads a goods train over Vauxhall Bridge towards the station during the 1960s. The poster is a reminder of Yarmouth's holiday industry, and Mike and Bernie Winters, Joe Henderson and Mike Yarwood were amongst the household names billed to appear at the Britannia Pier Theatre that summer. (Railway Record of the British Isles)

63. With the obligatory flagman striding out ahead of it, a train for the docks has just crossed Vauxhall Bridge and approaches North Quay Junction, again during the 1960s. The long shadows and empty streets are a reminder that this train often set out on its journey long before the holidaymakers were sitting down to breakfast in their boarding houses. (I.C.Allen/Transport Treasury)

64. This is North Quay Junction around 1960: just a set of points embedded in the tarmac road surface. The line to the left heads for a coal yard on the south bank of the Bure, that in the centre crosses Vauxhall bridge, whilst the right hand fork, underneath the lorry, is the Yarmouth Union line. (NRS Archive)

YARMOUTH TRAMWAYS

The speed of locomotives along the tramways must not exceed **six miles per hour**, and the speed through facing points, whether fixed or moveable, must not exceed **four miles per hour**.

The speed must not exceed **four miles per hour** from a point 220 yards on the Vauxhall Station side of the prolongation of the centre line of the Haven Bridge over the River Yare to the end of the tramways at the fish wharf.

The speed must not exceed **two miles per hour** for a distance of 30 yards on each side of the prolongation of the centre line of the Haven Bridge.

Each locomotive must be preceded at a distance of about ten yards by a person exhibiting a red flag by day and a red light by night; when a train is being shunted and the locomotive is in rear, the person must precede the foremost wagon and exhibit the signals as herein directed for the locomotive.

The Driver must act under the instructions of the Shunter.

The locomotive will work all wagons direct to and from Vauxhall yard over the Bure Bridge and a brake van must be in the rear in each direction accompanied by a Shunter.

(From British Railways Sectional Appendix 1972.)

65. Until the M&GN line closed in February 1959, White Swan yard was serviced from Beach station, with two daily return trips shown in the working timetable right up to the end. Class J68 0-6-0T no. 68651 has worked round from Beach station during the mid 1950s, and stands astride a level crossing during the shunting operations. A railwayman, lorry driver and the inevitable small boy look on. (I.C.Allen/Transport Treasury)

YARMOUTH UNION LINE.

Before any shunting is performed in the White Swan yard "No Man's Gates" **must be** locked against the public. The tram foreman will be held responsible for securing the gates, and guards must not commence shunting until the foreman arrives and the gates are locked.

(From M&GN Appendix 1918.)

66. Once the M&GN line had closed, trains reached the yard from the North Quay Junction direction. After running through the streets for some distance, they squeezed through what was known as the "Hole in the Wall", a narrow gap next to the public house which gave the yard its name. During the 1960s, a diesel shunter waits to enter the grass grown yard. (I.C.Allen/Transport Treasury)

67. At much the same time, a diesel shunter busies itself amongst the weeds and the litter in the yard. Coal, seen here both loose and sacked, was the reason for the line's survival until 1970. In 2009 the White Swan pub was still standing, but building development had removed most traces of the railway. (I.C.Allen/Transport Treasury)

68. Back at North Quay Junction, we find that a goods train returning from the docks has encountered a problem. There are tales of the train crew manhandling parked cars off the tracks, but the Birds Eye lorry is a different proposition altogether.
(I.C.Allen/
Transport Treasury)

➔ 69. The man in the front cab surveys the scene as class Y10 0-4-0T no 8403 makes its way along Hall Quay around 1950. For over 40 years, trains over the quay lines were horse-drawn and it was not until the 1880s that steam traction appeared. The first locomotives used were 0-4-0 tram engines of what became LNER class Y6, and these were later supplemented by the externally similar J70 0-6-0s. Usage of the tram engines declined after the two Y10s were introduced in 1930. These double ended Sentinel locomotives were a common sight on the dock lines until no.8403 was withdrawn in 1952, having outlasted its sister by some four years. (R.J.Adderson collection)

➔ 70. Approaching Hall Quay, the enginemen are keeping a sharp look out on either side as a train bound for the docks disrupts the traffic flow at what is arguably the town's busiest road junction. 204 hp diesel shunters such as this, with their motion obscured by protective skirting, and cowcatchers front and rear, first appeared on the quay lines in 1952.
(I.C.Allen/Transport Treasury)

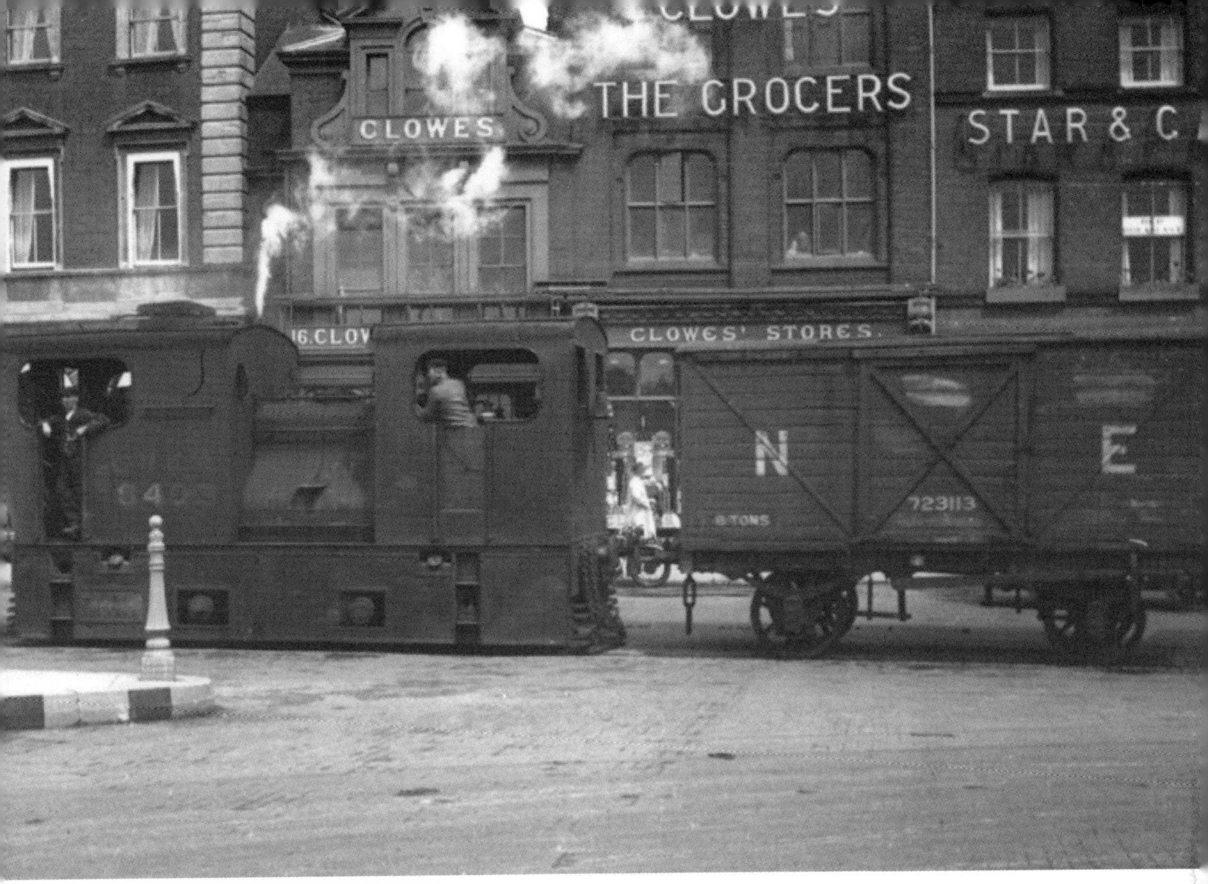
THE GROCERS
CLOWES
CLOWES' STORES.
N
E
723113

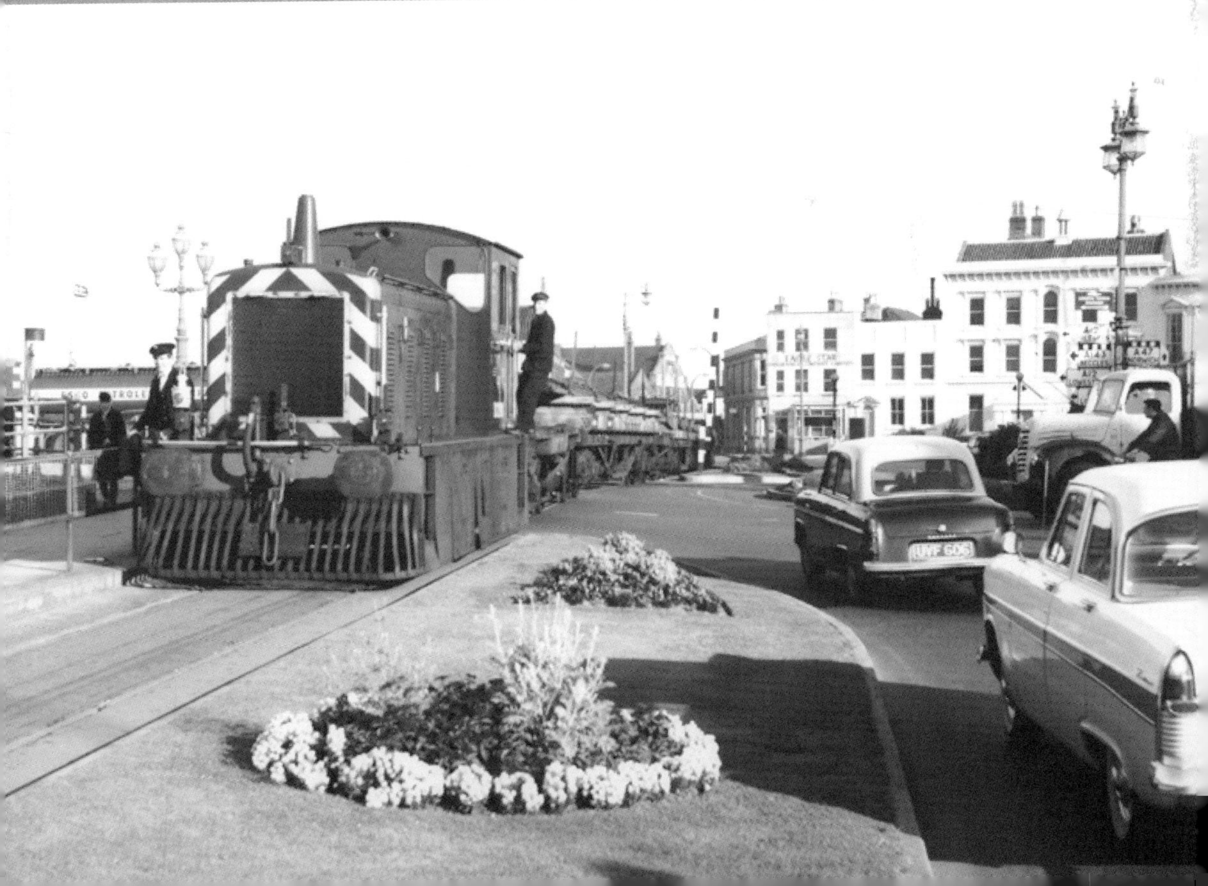
UWF 606

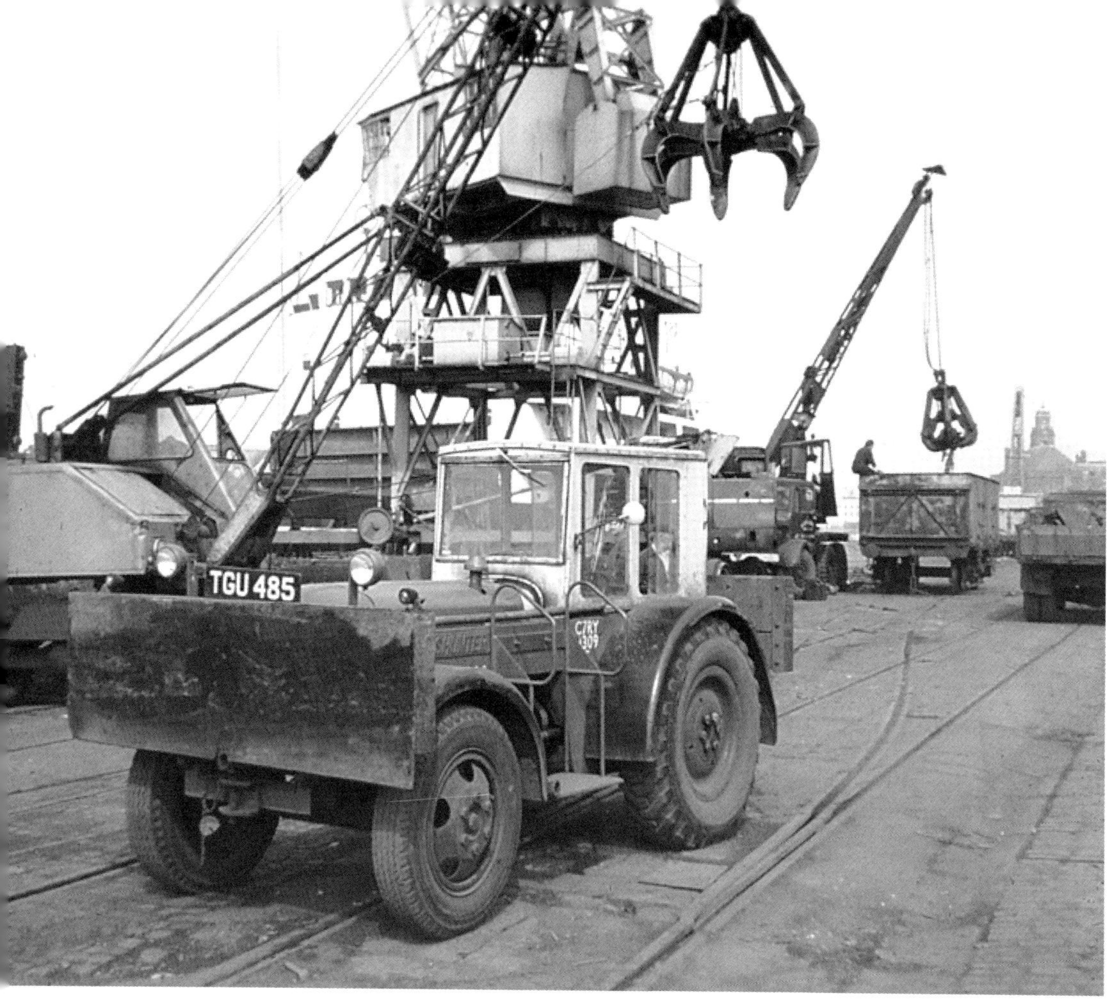
TGU 485

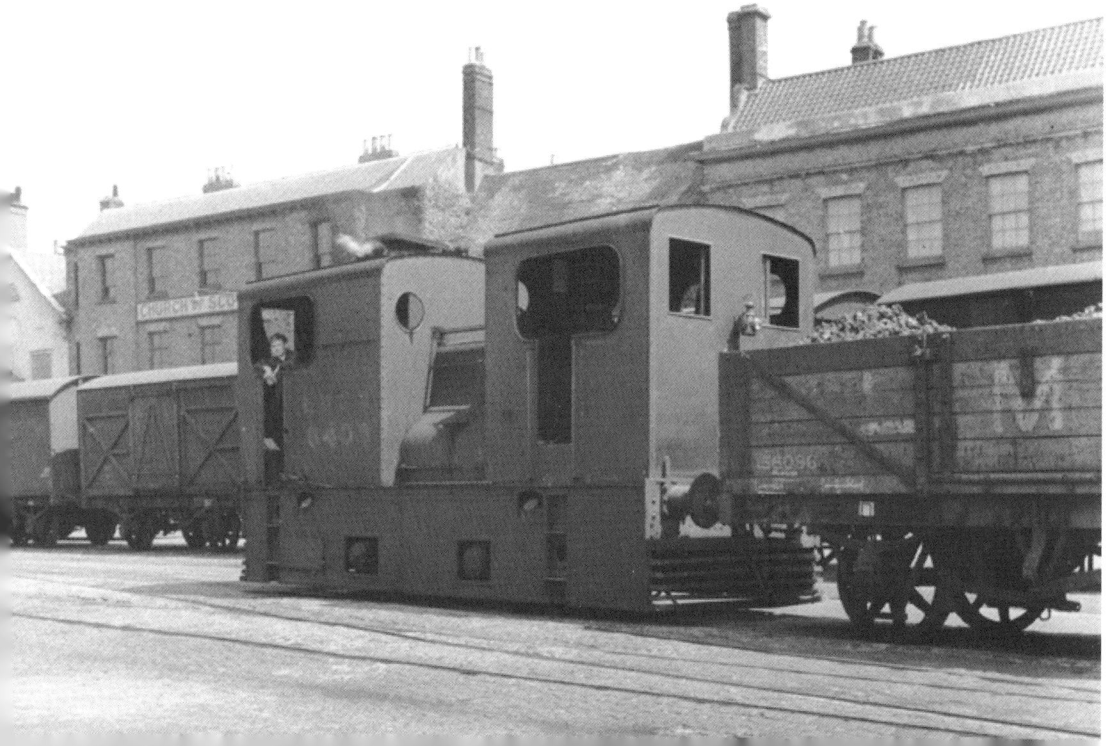

← 71. The sheer novelty of the street running means that photographs of trains on the quay lines are not uncommon, but few photographers even noticed the tractor which shunted wagons around on the quayside. An "Epping Auto-Shunter" stands amid the cranes on South Quay on 18th April 1968. The massive beams at each end are at the level of wagon buffers, while a platform for the shunter, complete with handrails, is fixed between the wheels. (G.H.Smith)

← 72. Sentinel no. 8403 is shunting on South Quay on 17th June 1938. The buildings beyond were still recognizable in 2009, the one to the right housing the Norfolk Nelson Museum. However, there was no trace of the rails set in the quayside, as the area has undergone a facelift since the railway closed in 1975. (M.Yarwood / GW Trust collection)

73. The line was extended beyond South Quay in 1867 to cater for the heavy traffic expected from the new Fish Wharf. We are looking northwards along the railway, with the extensive Fish Wharf buildings stretching away on the left. This picture dates from around 1960, when the North Sea fishing industry was in terminal decline. (NRS Archive)

3. Reedham to Lowestoft
REEDHAM SWING BRIDGE

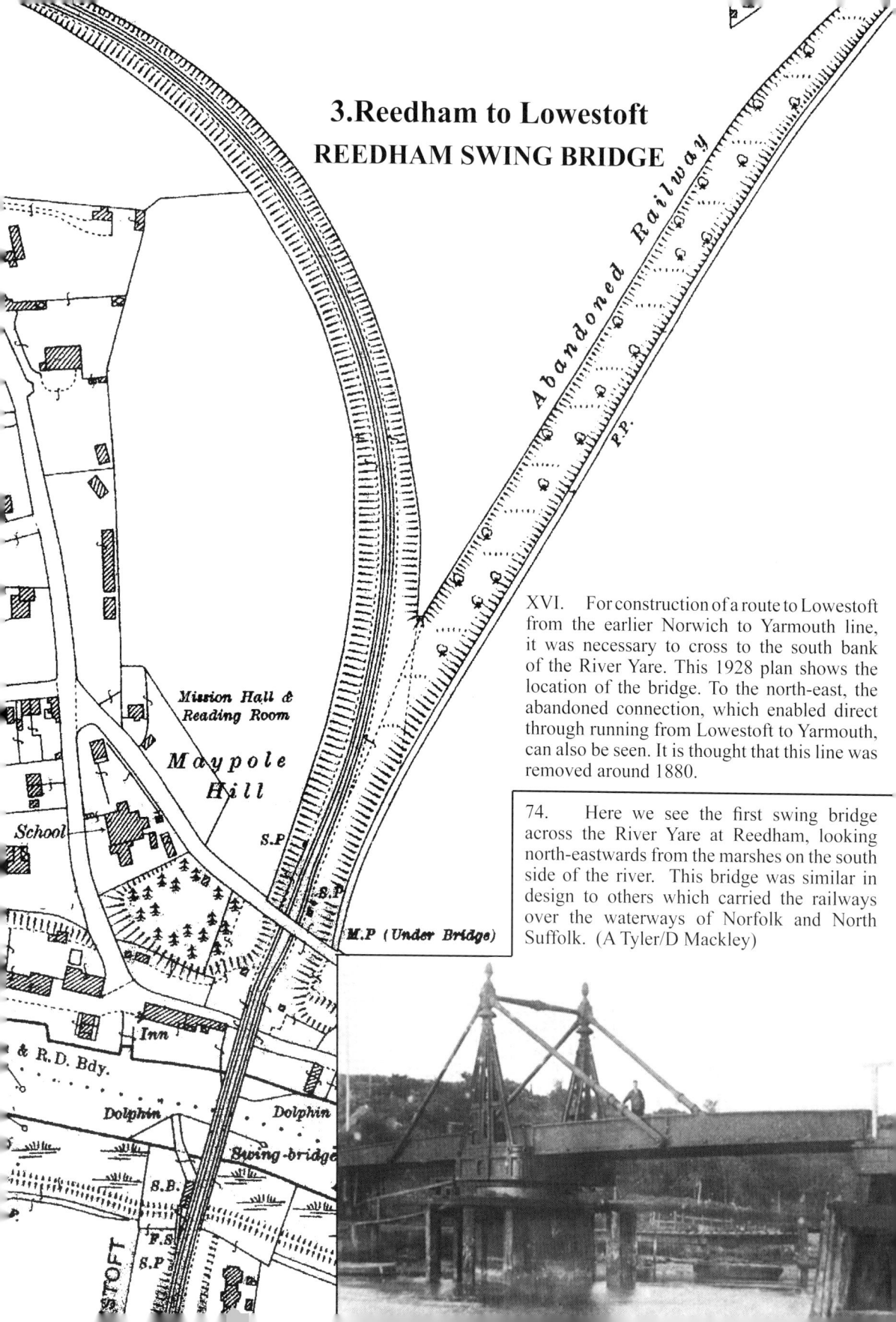

XVI. For construction of a route to Lowestoft from the earlier Norwich to Yarmouth line, it was necessary to cross to the south bank of the River Yare. This 1928 plan shows the location of the bridge. To the north-east, the abandoned connection, which enabled direct through running from Lowestoft to Yarmouth, can also be seen. It is thought that this line was removed around 1880.

74. Here we see the first swing bridge across the River Yare at Reedham, looking north-eastwards from the marshes on the south side of the river. This bridge was similar in design to others which carried the railways over the waterways of Norfolk and North Suffolk. (A Tyler/D Mackley)

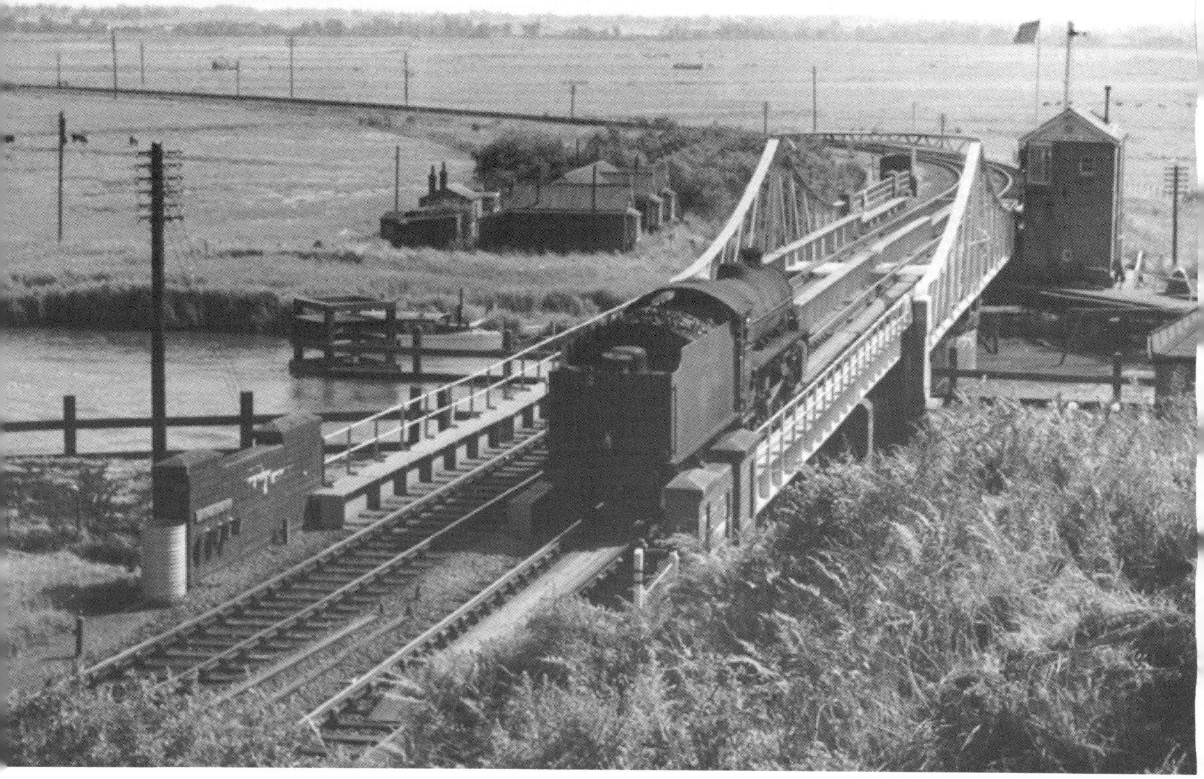

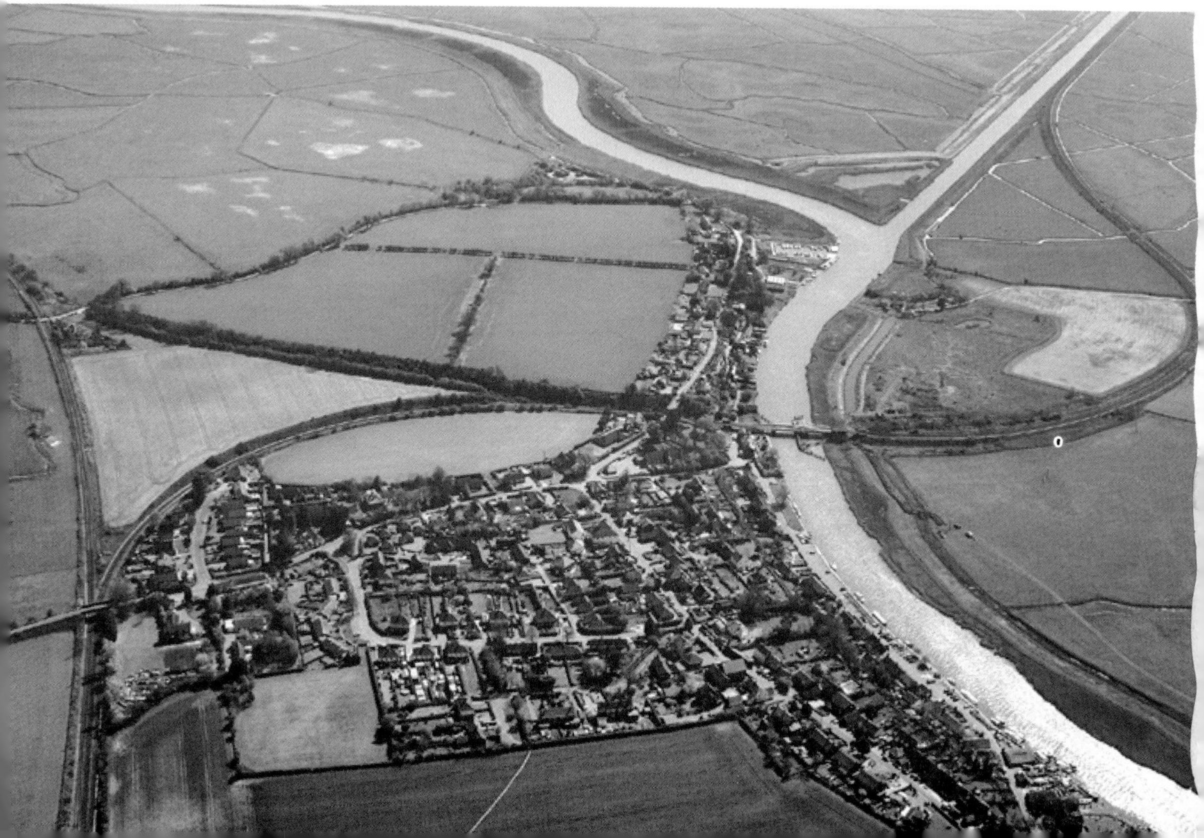

75.   A goods train crosses the old bridge in 1904, dwarfed by construction work on the replacement structure. One of the sections of the new bridge is in the centre of the picture, supported on cradles which will enable it to be rolled into position when required. Most of the workers appear to be busy on the framework of the swinging span on the far side of the river. The formation for the double track is complete, and in the foreground the cutting has been widened for the new alignment of the railway. We are looking southwards from the road bridge, a location which still provided a panoramic view of the bridge a century later. (R.J.Adderson collection)

76.   A tug makes its way down river with a string of empty barges during the inter-war years. The bridge is set against river traffic, so the crew must have lowered the tall funnel in order to pass underneath it. A pleasure steamer is close to the north bank of the river, waiting its turn to negotiate the bridge to reach Reedham Quay. This aspect of the bridge and signal box had changed little in 2009, but by then commercial river traffic was very much a thing of the past. (P.Standley collection)

← 77. The viewpoint here is almost identical to that used in picture 75, as a class B1 4-6-0 crosses the bridge in 1960, running tender-first towards Norwich. Opposite the signal box is an isolated row of small cottages, of basically corrugated iron construction. (M.Fordham)

↙ 78. This aerial view dating from 2007 emphasises the sinuous course of the Lowestoft line as it describes an S-bend to cross the River Yare and to link up with the Yarmouth line at the extreme left of the picture. In the early days another line allowed direct running between Yarmouth and Lowestoft without reversal at the station. This was not used by timetabled passenger trains, and although the tracks have been lifted for well over a century, the tree-lined cutting of this third side of the triangle is clearly defined. At the top right, the New Cut heads directly south-eastwards to Haddiscoe, parting company with the winding course of the Yare. (M.Page)

WEST OF HADDISCOE

79. The two mile stretch of railway alongside the New Cut is vulnerable to flooding, with consequent disruption to train services. On one such occasion a gang of workmen pause from their repair work for a group photograph. For the moment, the damage will not get any worse, as large numbers of sandbags have sealed the breach in the bank. This picture was taken in the aftermath of the 1953 floods, when the line between Reedham and Lowestoft was out of action for some 12 days. (G.L.Kenworthy collection)

80. When the railway took over the New Cut, it also inherited the lifting bridge which carried the Yarmouth to Beccles road over the waterway. Here a broads cruiser negotiates the bridge around 1960, with the replacement road bridge beginning to take shape on the north bank of the Cut. Visible for miles around, the new concrete structure had none of the rattling charm of its flimsy predecessor. It also spanned the railway, allowing the level crossing next to the first station to be abolished. (M.Page)

81. The new bridge provides a fine view of the railway and New Cut as they run straight and parallel through the countryside. We are looking in a north-westerly direction as no.47810 heads for the coast with a train of main line coaches on 28th July 2006. This is an additional working from Norwich to cater for the crowds attending the Lowestoft Air Show. (S.Goodrum)

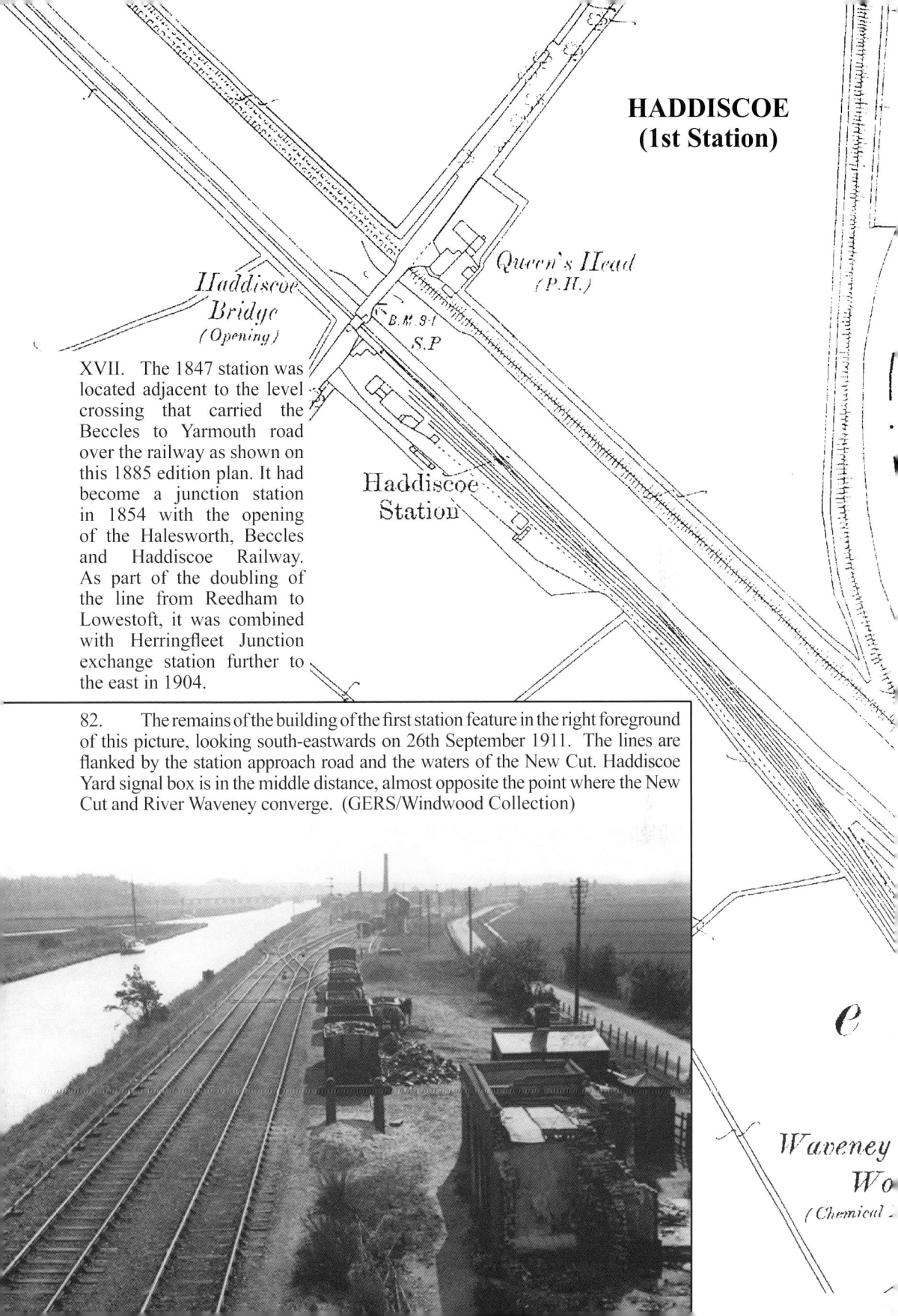

HADDISCOE
(1st Station)

XVII. The 1847 station was located adjacent to the level crossing that carried the Beccles to Yarmouth road over the railway as shown on this 1885 edition plan. It had become a junction station in 1854 with the opening of the Halesworth, Beccles and Haddiscoe Railway. As part of the doubling of the line from Reedham to Lowestoft, it was combined with Herringfleet Junction exchange station further to the east in 1904.

82. The remains of the building of the first station feature in the right foreground of this picture, looking south-eastwards on 26th September 1911. The lines are flanked by the station approach road and the waters of the New Cut. Haddiscoe Yard signal box is in the middle distance, almost opposite the point where the New Cut and River Waveney converge. (GERS/Windwood Collection)

**HADDISCOE
(2nd Station)**

XVIII. Having opened in 1859 as Herringfleet Junction exchange station with a platform to the east of the East Suffolk line, opportunity was taken to combine the stations in 1904 as mentioned earlier. Part of the work also entailed providing a new access road across the marshes for the inhabitants of the village of Haddiscoe, over a mile to the south-west; the start of this road can be seen to the left of Haddiscoe Junction on this 1905 plan. This location was also covered in our earlier volume *Saxmundham to Yarmouth*.

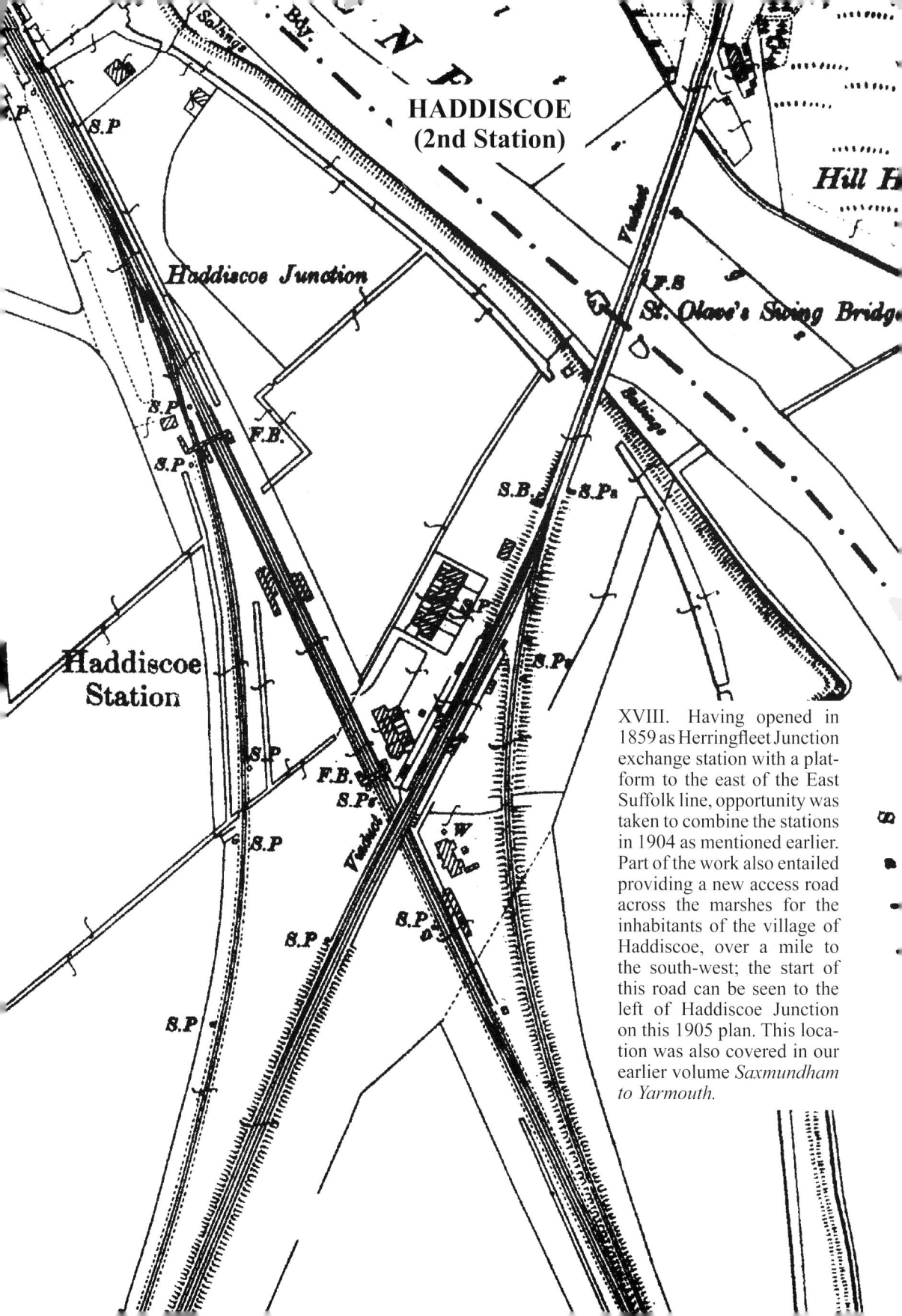

83. The booking office was not on the platforms but alongside the road approach to the station. Access to the platforms in 1911 was by means of this rather fine covered footbridge, the right hand span of which passed over the connecting spur to Fleet Junction on the East Suffolk line. The High Level platforms are in the centre of the picture, between the cottages and the footbridge.
(GERS/
Windwood Collection)

84. Looking east in Great Eastern Railway days, we see a train for Norwich approaching the station, with its matching pair of waiting rooms. The enamel running in board proclaims the station name in the standard GER lettering style, and to the right of this is the embankment topped by the High Level station.
(Lens of Sutton Collection)

85. There was another footbridge at the east end of the platforms, close to the girder bridge carrying the East Suffolk line. Class K3 2-6-0 no. 61981 passes under these bridges with a train of containers from Lowestoft during the late 1950s. The pedestrian passageway giving access to the southbound High Level platform is to the left of the locomotive.
(W.J.Naunton)

86. The curved and sharply graded line to Fleet Junction saw regular goods traffic but only the very occasional passenger train. Nonetheless a platform face was provided and, as we see here, a short length of this remained until the 1960s. Haddiscoe Junction signal box is to the extreme left of the picture. This achieved fame by becoming an exhibit at the Science Museum in London before moving on again to Mangapps Farm Museum in Essex in 1996. (NRS Archive)

87. Although the station is unstaffed, the waiting rooms are looking very smart on 19th March 1967, and appear to have received a fresh coat of paint. New electric lights have been provided, but one of the old lamp holders remains in place on the down platform. The East Suffolk bridge had been demolished after the High Level line was closed in November 1959, and just the abutments remain. (Railway Record of the British Isles/G.L.Pring)

88. Another eight years have passed, and the station facilities have been reduced as passenger numbers declined. By May 1975 the buildings have been knocked down and the up platform has been shortened drastically. We are looking north-westwards with the abandoned platform of the High Level station in the foreground. (D.C.Pearce)

89. A view from the air in May 2007 reveals traces of former railway features that are not readily apparent from ground level. We are looking in a generally north-westerly direction, with the Lowestoft to Reedham line bisecting the picture. The path of the East Suffolk line from Yarmouth is marked by the piers of the old swing bridge and then the High Level signal box, before it crosses the surviving line. To the west a curving line of trees shows the alignment of the spur to Fleet Junction, although buildings have obliterated the site of the junction itself. On the opposite side of the line, more trees mark the course of the east to north spur from Marsh Junction to the High Level line. (M.Page)

90. In 1989 there was yet another change to the platform arrangement, when the short section of the up platform shown in picture 88 was abandoned. It was replaced by an entirely new structure, standing where the line to Fleet Junction once diverged. A train from Lowestoft speeds past on 13th June 2009. The full length of the down platform is still maintained for access to the houses to the east of the line. (R.J.Adderson)

WEST OF SOMERLEYTON

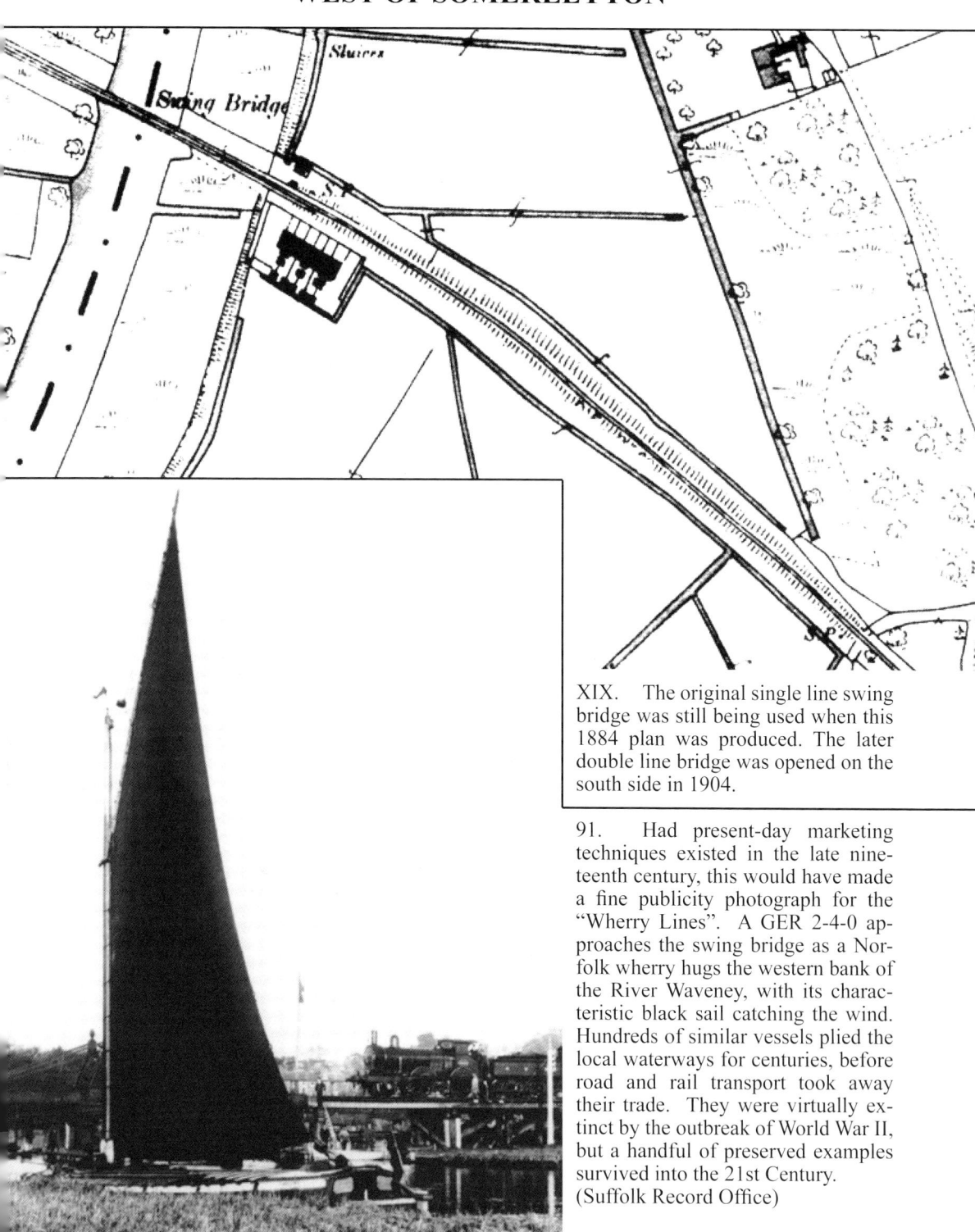

XIX. The original single line swing bridge was still being used when this 1884 plan was produced. The later double line bridge was opened on the south side in 1904.

91. Had present-day marketing techniques existed in the late nineteenth century, this would have made a fine publicity photograph for the "Wherry Lines". A GER 2-4-0 approaches the swing bridge as a Norfolk wherry hugs the western bank of the River Waveney, with its characteristic black sail catching the wind. Hundreds of similar vessels plied the local waterways for centuries, before road and rail transport took away their trade. They were virtually extinct by the outbreak of World War II, but a handful of preserved examples survived into the 21st Century. (Suffolk Record Office)

92. In common with its counterpart at Reedham the original swing bridge was replaced in 1904 by a more modern structure carrying double-track. A century or so later, a class 170 rumbles over the bridge as it heads for Lowestoft. (M.Page)

G. E. R.

From

TO

SOMERLEYTON

SOMERLEYTON

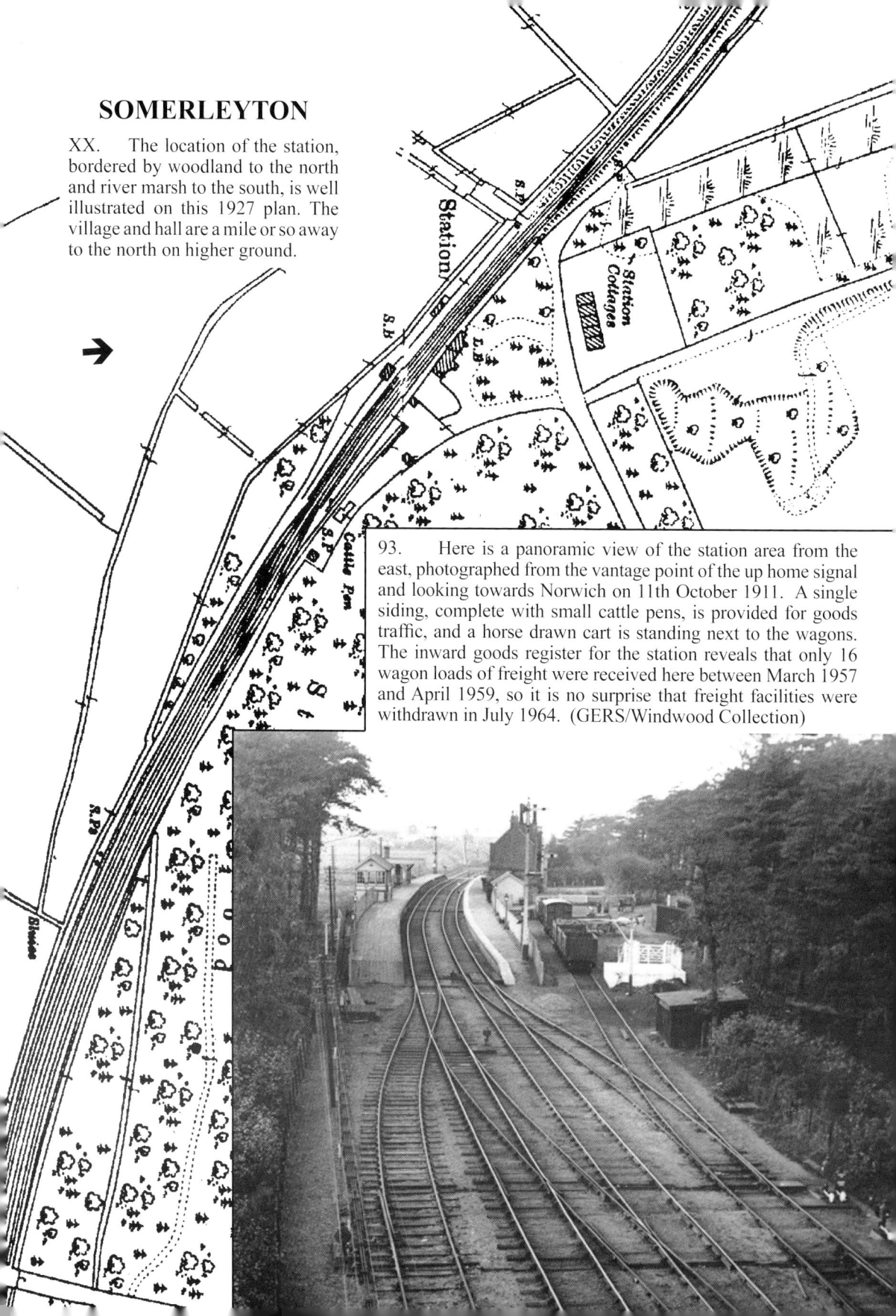

XX. The location of the station, bordered by woodland to the north and river marsh to the south, is well illustrated on this 1927 plan. The village and hall are a mile or so away to the north on higher ground.

93. Here is a panoramic view of the station area from the east, photographed from the vantage point of the up home signal and looking towards Norwich on 11th October 1911. A single siding, complete with small cattle pens, is provided for goods traffic, and a horse drawn cart is standing next to the wagons. The inward goods register for the station reveals that only 16 wagon loads of freight were received here between March 1957 and April 1959, so it is no surprise that freight facilities were withdrawn in July 1964. (GERS/Windwood Collection)

94. A postcard from much the same era provides more detail of the station itself, with the lines curving away towards Lowestoft beyond the platform ends. The station signal box is behind the waiting shelter on the up platform. Five of the six men on the opposite platform are in railway uniform, which reminds us just how many people found employment on the railway, even in rural areas such as this. (Lens of Sutton Collection)

95. The main station building was much grander than those at other locations on the line. This is explained by the fact that the station served Somerleyton Hall, which was for some years the home of Samuel Morton Peto, one of the promoters of the railway and a major entrepreneur of his day. Our view of the building, seen from the approach road on 29th August 1971, emphasizes the ornate architectural style. (Railway Record of the British Isles/G.L.Pring)

96. Two passengers are waiting for the train from Norwich as it runs into the station on 13th June 2009. The station building continues to dominate the scene, although it is no longer in railway use, and lost its canopy back in 1971. Train movements are still controlled by semaphore signals, which have been worked from the signal box at the Swing Bridge since 1965, when the station signal box was abolished. (R.J.Adderson)

→ XXI. The original station, named Mutford, was opened as a single platform to the west of the level crossing. Renamed Oulton Broad (Mutford) in 1881, the suffix was dropped in 1915 and "North" was added in 1927, shortly after the survey date of this plan. In the meantime, the station had been rebuilt as a double platform to the east of the level crossing in 1901 in connection with the doubling of the original single line; the goods yard on the north side of the line was provided at the same time. Prior to the provision in 1901 of the double junction shown to the east of the station, the two single lines from Beccles and Reedham merely ran parallel to each other before joining at Coke Ovens Junction, a few hundred yards from Lowestoft station. The junction was altered again in 1986 in connection with the introduction of radio signalling on the East Suffolk line.

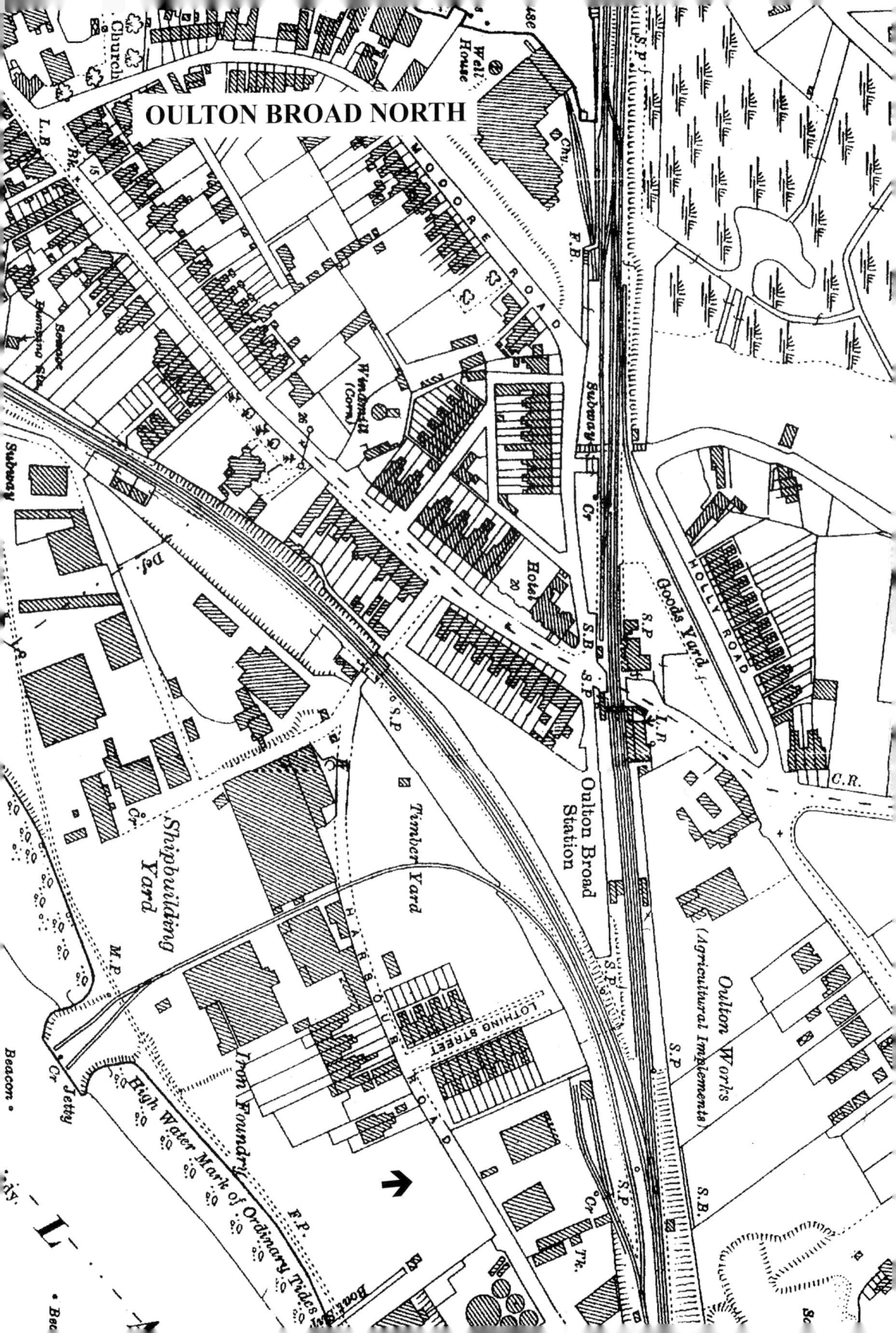

OULTON BROAD NORTH

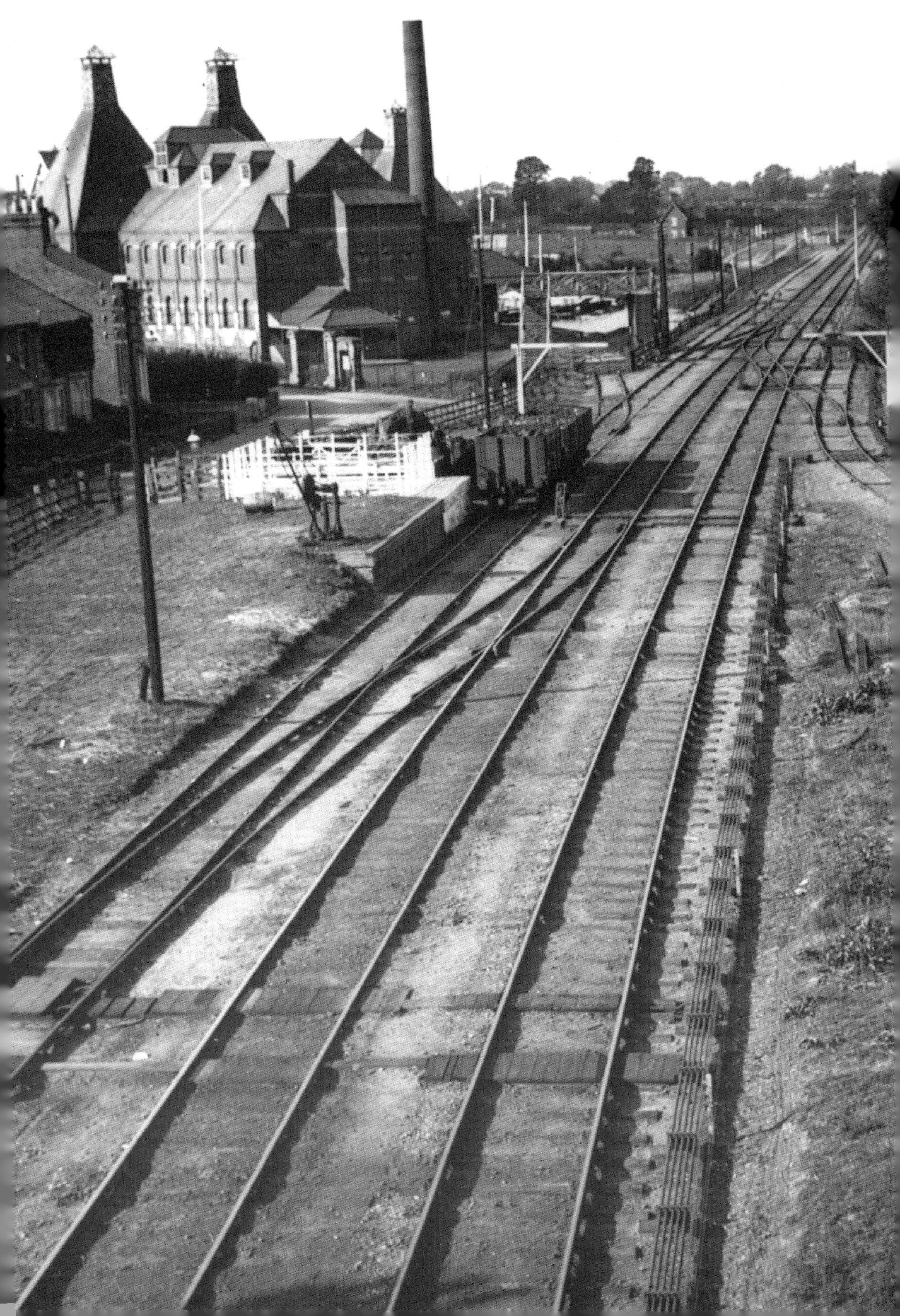

97. Even as early as 1911, the urban approach to Oulton Broad marked the end of the largely deserted countryside through which the railway has run since leaving Brundall. Here we are looking towards Norwich, with sidings to both right and left of the running lines. The compact goods facility, incorporating cattle pens, loading dock and a small fixed crane, could provide inspiration to railway modellers. Over to the left is a large maltings building, which was served by a private siding. (GERS/Windwood Collection)

98. This is the view in the opposite direction, towards the distant station, again on 11th October 1911. A small timber footbridge on brick abutments spans the private siding to the maltings, and the complexity of the track layout is noteworthy. (GERS/Windwood Collection)

99.   We are looking towards Norwich from the platform at Oulton Broad North station on 29th August 1971. A "bus shelter" type building has replaced an earlier brick built waiting room on this platform, but the main building is much as it had been for many years. The signal stands out against the white sighting board, which was provided for clearer visibility against the background of the footbridge. (Railway Record of the British Isles/G.L.Pring)

100.   A class 156 in National Express livery runs into the station in April 2009. The surroundings have changed only in detail since the previous picture. Perhaps the most obvious change is the removal of the footbridge, which allows us a clearer view of the signal box. Oddly, the signal retains its sighting board, even though the cluttered background is no more. The level crossing gates have also gone, replaced by barriers, which remain a cause for complaint from impatient motorists on what is a very busy road. (G.L.Kenworthy)

101. No. 170201 accelerates away from the station on the last leg of its journey from Norwich on 16th June 2009. It is passing the simplified junction with the East Suffolk line, which curves away to the south. A contrasting picture of this location as it was in 1911 appears in *Branch Lines around Lowestoft*. (R.J.Adderson)

LOWESTOFT CENTRAL

XXIII. This plan shows the situation in the immediate vicinity of the station as it existed in 1904 and is at a scale of aproximately 15ins. to 1 mile. The various associated railway locations that were no longer used, or had disappeared, by 2009 were illustrated in our earlier volume *Branch Lines Around Lowestoft*.

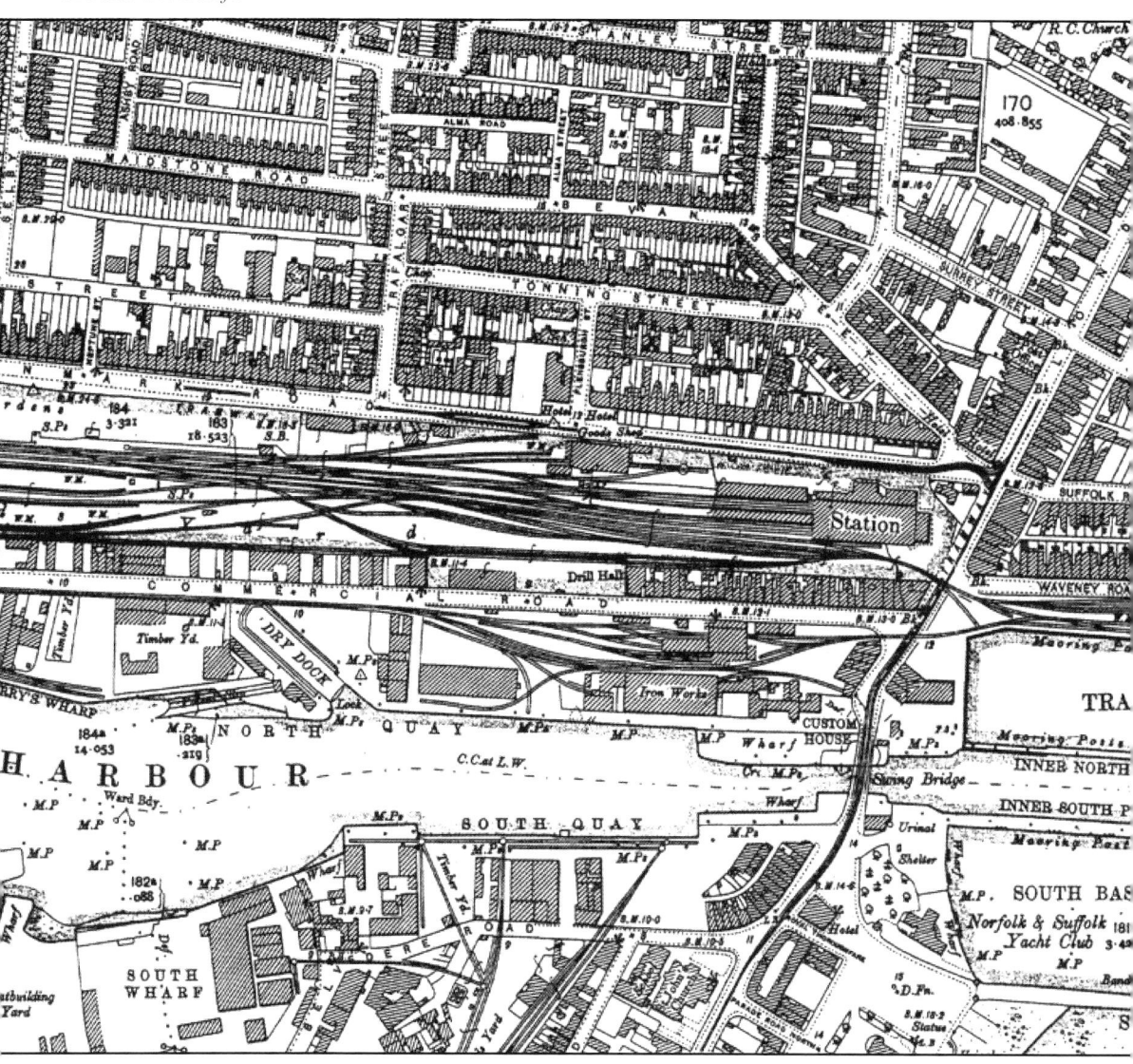

102. A signal gantry on the approach to the station produces a fine silhouette against the eastern sky as the lamp man goes about his duties in the early years of the twentieth century.
(G.L.Kenworthy collection)

103. This is the exterior of the station building, seen from the south-east at much the same time. A Great Eastern Railway bus, operating the service to Southwold, stands in the forecourt, whilst the tracks of the Corporation tramway system are set in the road surface in the foreground.
(Lens of Sutton Collection)

104. Before the diesels came, local trains could be dingy in the extreme. This, though, is an exception to the rule, as a shining class A5 4-6-2T no. 69824 sets out for Norwich with three new and equally clean Mk 1 coaches during the mid 1950s. (I.C.Allen/Transport Treasury)

105. A display of tulips brightened up the concourse in April 1954. Shielded from the elements by the station roof, the flowers would have been dependent on regular visits from the railwayman and his watering can. A typical 1950s family poses for a cameraman from the local newspaper, while the W. H. Smith bookstall in the background has a wide range of papers and magazines on show. (Archant Norwich)

106. By 1969 the flowerbed had gone, replaced by a far more practical, if less colourful, timetable display. In front of this is the squat form of one of the mechanical gadgets that so impressed children of the pre-computer age. First you put your money in the slot, and then by turning a handle to the appropriate letters or numbers on the dial, you could spell out your name, address, or any other message, which would eventually emerge from the innards of the machine stamped on a thin strip of metal. The timber roof beams are again prominent, and a comparison with the previous picture reveals that additional supports have been deemed necessary. Parcels traffic was still heavy at this time, if the trolleys at the back of the concourse are any guide. (British Railways)

107. The wooden roof extended out onto both platforms, providing shelter for passengers joining and leaving trains. Even from a distance, the scale of these awnings and stanchions is apparent, as we look across the neglected trackwork to the south of the station in July 1966. From this area a single line crossed the main road and headed out eastwards to the fish wharf, just to the right of the three-storey building in the distance. (Railway Record of the British Isles/G.L.Pring)

108. Seen from the north-east in September 1969, the exterior of the station building had changed little, when compared with picture 103. The main entrance to the station is beneath the awning on the north side. Remarkably the blue enamel "British Railways Lowestoft Central" sign was still attached to the frontage forty years later, unaffected by the corporate British Rail era and the successive train operators following privatisation. (British Railways)

109. The platform awnings were cut back during the late 1960s, although the roof over the concourse remained. This was the scene on 27th August 1985, with a class 101 waiting at the exposed platform. The rarely-used lines to the south of the station are atypically busy, hosting a class 31 with a goods train for Norwich and a track maintenance machine. (S.McNae)

↓ 110. Although general goods traffic had ceased, occasional freight trains could be seen into the 21st century. These brought a waste product of the North Sea drilling operation from Aberdeen to Lowestoft for treatment. No 37682 *Hartlepool Pipe Mill* waits to leave with a train of empties returning to Scotland on 18th December 1998. Little track rationalisation had taken place, and even ten years later the rail approach to the town was characterised by expanses of rarely used trackwork. (R.J.Adderson)

111. No. 156412 waits to leave for Norwich on July 9th 2009, whilst 170207 stands in platform 2 on an East Suffolk line service. The overall roof had been demolished in 1992, leaving the concourse and platforms open to the elements. It was sorely missed on Summer days such as this. (R.J.Adderson)

Local timetable August 1930.

4. Brundall to Breydon Junction.
LINGWOOD

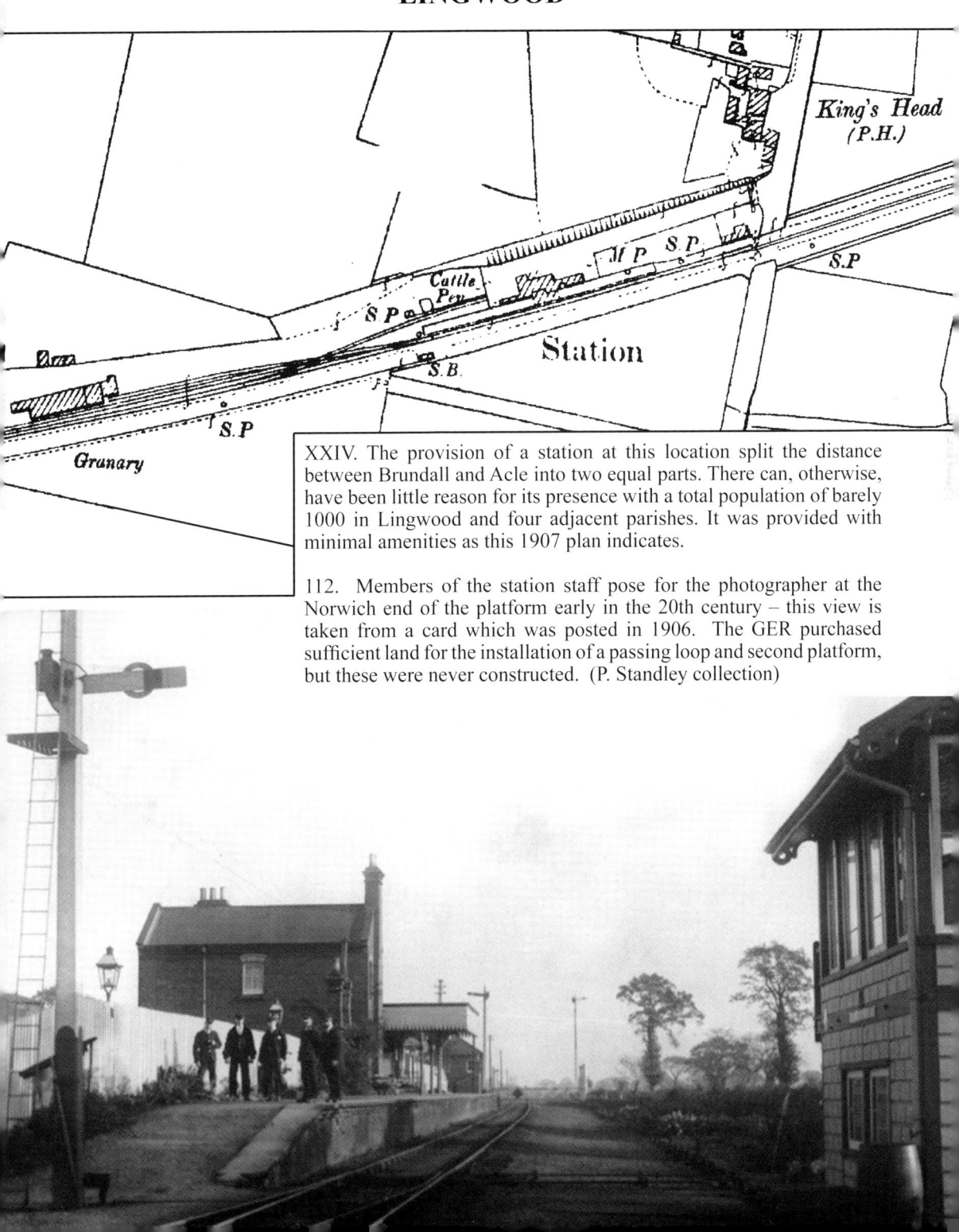

XXIV. The provision of a station at this location split the distance between Brundall and Acle into two equal parts. There can, otherwise, have been little reason for its presence with a total population of barely 1000 in Lingwood and four adjacent parishes. It was provided with minimal amenities as this 1907 plan indicates.

112. Members of the station staff pose for the photographer at the Norwich end of the platform early in the 20th century – this view is taken from a card which was posted in 1906. The GER purchased sufficient land for the installation of a passing loop and second platform, but these were never constructed. (P. Standley collection)

113. The goods shed and yard must be amongst the least photographed features of Norfolk's railways. Here they are on a bleak November day in 1966, goods facilities having been withdrawn some three months previously, on 1st August. An empty lamp overlooks the scene, with a totem sign attached to the old rail which acts as the lamp post.
(Railway Record of the British Isles/G.L.Pring)

114. No 31416 approaches the station from the east on 21st June 1986, heading a Summer Saturday train from Yarmouth to Liverpool. The ground frame hut, in the style of a miniature signalbox, is dwarfed by the locomotive and looks oddly out of scale. It is said that this once served a similar function at Martham on the M&GN and old photographs suggest that the structure there was indeed very similar. (R.J. Adderson)

115. Two passengers look on as their train runs into the platform on 12th September 1992. Although unstaffed, the station is still very tidy, with a freshly painted canopy and flowers brightening the scene. In 2009 the station building provided Bed & Breakfast accommodation, and the proprietor continued to tend the flower tubs on the platform, maintaining the time-honoured floral tradition of the country railway station. (D.C.Pearce)

G. E. R.

Lingwood

ACLE

116. We are looking south-westwards from the station footbridge during the late 1960s. There is still some goods traffic in the yard, which was closed in February 1969, and the rail entrance to the large goods shed has been bricked up. The loop was extended in 1960, allowing two lengthy loco-hauled trains to pass each other. (Railway Record of the British Isles/G.L.Pring)

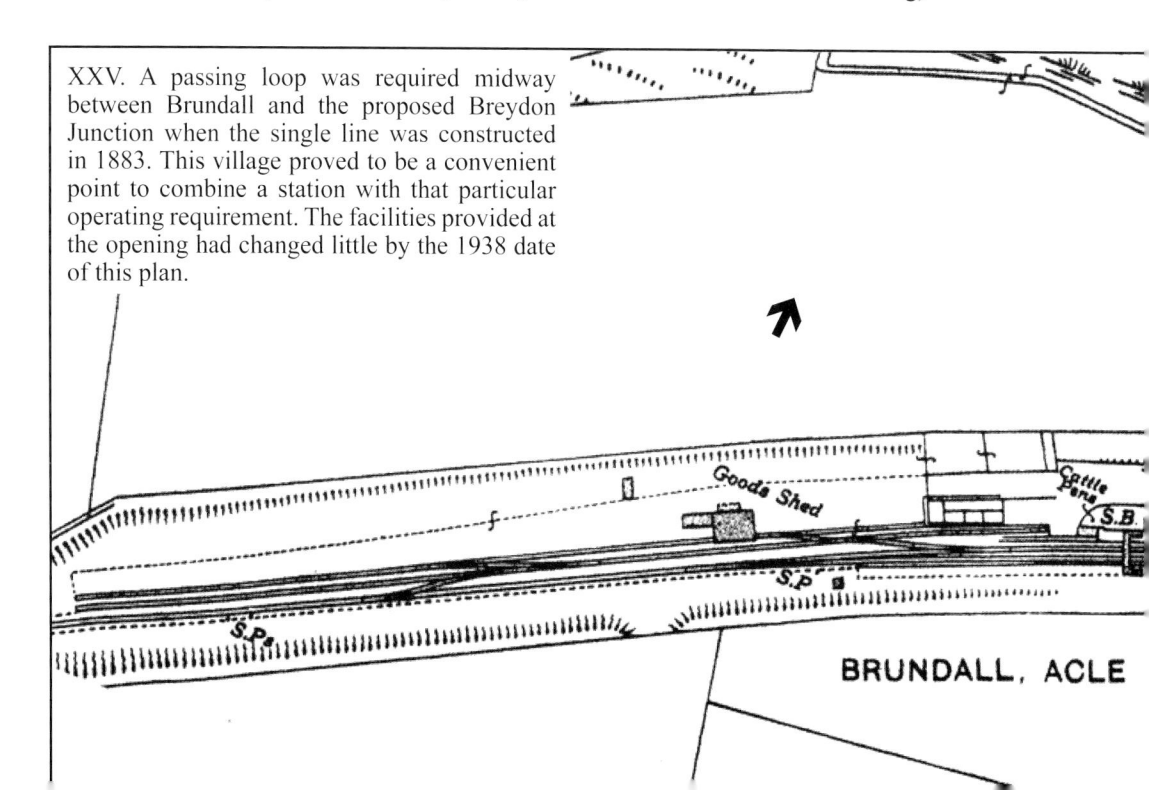

XXV. A passing loop was required midway between Brundall and the proposed Breydon Junction when the single line was constructed in 1883. This village proved to be a convenient point to combine a station with that particular operating requirement. The facilities provided at the opening had changed little by the 1938 date of this plan.

BRUNDALL, ACLE

117. Two class 25 diesels power through the station with a Summer Saturday train from Yarmouth to Derby on 16th August 1980. To the delight of local enthusiasts, this class of engine made regular visits to the area with holiday trains such as this for some 15 years. (R.J.Adderson)

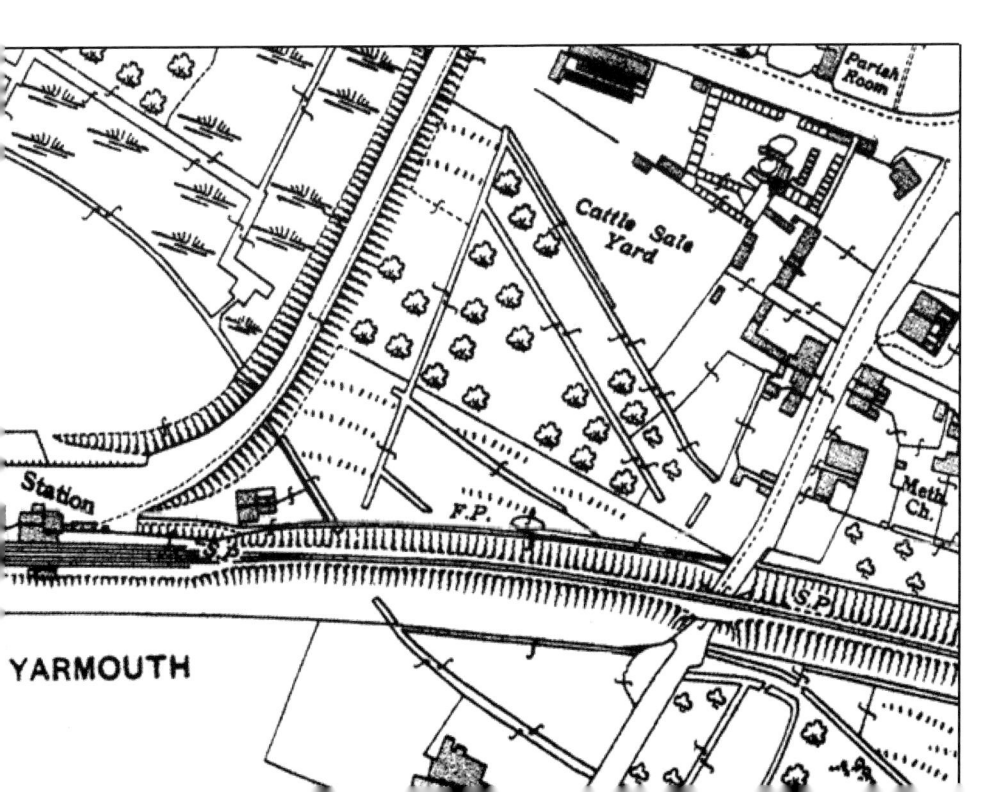

YARMOUTH

118. A Cravens DMU stands in the morning sunshine on 29th August 1981. Passengers on the opposite platform are waiting for an up train, and the unit will be able to resume its journey to Yarmouth as soon as this has cleared the single track. (R.Powell)

119. Two class 156s pass in the station on 18th June 2009. The footbridge, signal box, and station building combine to create something of a traditional scene. At the time this was one of just three occasions each day when trains were timetabled to pass here. The viewpoint is the bridge spanning the tracks at the west end of the station. This had been built in the late 1980s to carry a new road. (R.J.Adderson)

EAST OF ACLE

120.   Beyond Acle, the line runs through a broad expanse of marshland before joining up with the line from Reedham at Breydon Junction. Although the landscape is similar to that on the Berney Arms route, the sense of isolation is less as the busy A47 road runs parallel to the railway. Two Brush Type 2 diesel locomotives and a class B1 4-6-0 pass the windpump at Stracey Arms during the Summer of 1960. They are returning to Norwich after working trains down to Yarmouth, which lies some five miles away, beyond the distant horizon. (M.Fordham)

EAST ANGLIA PAYTRAINS

THE WHERRY
Norwich-Yarmouth-Lowestoft

5 May 1975 — 2 May 1976

Middleton Press

Easebourne Lane, Midhurst, West Sussex. GU29 9AZ Tel:01730 813169

www.middletonpress.co.uk email:info@middletonpress.co.uk
A-978 0 906520 B- 978 1 873793 C- 978 1 901706 D-978 1 904474
E- 978 1 906008 F- 978 1 908174

EVOLVING THE ULTIMATE RAIL ENCYCLOPEDIA

All titles listed below were in print at time of publication - please check current availability by looking at our website - *www.middletonpress.co.uk* or by requesting a Brochure which includes our LATEST RAILWAY TITLES also our TRAMWAY, TROLLEYBUS, MILITARY and WATERWAYS series

A
Abergavenny to Merthyr C 91 8
Abertillery & Ebbw Vale Lines D 84 5
Aberystwyth to Carmarthen E 90 1
Allhallows - Branch Line to A 62 8
Alton - Branch Lines to A 11 6
Andover to Southampton A 82 6
Ascot - Branch Lines around A 64 2
Ashburton - Branch Line to B 95 4
Ashford - Steam to Eurostar B 67 1
Ashford to Dover A 48 2
Austrian Narrow Gauge D 04 3
Avonmouth - BL around D 42 5
Aylesbury to Rugby D 91 3

B
Baker Street to Uxbridge D 90 6
Bala to Llandudno E 87 1
Banbury to Birmingham D 27 2
Banbury to Cheltenham E 63 5
Bangor to Holyhead F 01 7
Bangor to Portmadoc E 72 7
Barking to Southend C 80 2
Barmouth to Pwllheli E 53 6
Barry - Branch Lines around D 50 0
Bath Green Park to Bristol C 36 9
Bath to Evercreech Junction A 60 4
Beamish 40 years on rails E94 9
Bedford to Wellingborough D 31 9
Birmingham to Wolverhampton E253
Bletchley to Cambridge D 94 4
Bletchley to Rugby E 07 9
Bodmin - Branch Lines around B 83 1
Bournemouth to Evercreech Jn A 46 8
Bournemouth to Weymouth A 57 4
Bradshaw's Guide 1866 F 05 5
Bradshaw's History F18 5
Bradshaw's Rail Times 1850 F 13 0
Bradshaw's Rail Times 1895 F 11 6
Branch Lines series - see town names
Brecon to Neath D 43 2
Brecon to Newport D 16 6
Brecon to Newtown E 06 2
Brighton to Eastbourne A 16 1
Brighton to Worthing A 03 1
Bromley South to Rochester B 23 7
Bromsgrove to Birmingham D 87 6
Bromsgrove to Gloucester D 73 9
Broxbourne to Cambridge F16 1
Brunel - A railtour D 74 6
Bude - Branch Line to B 29 9
Burnham to Evercreech Jn B 68 0

C
Cambridge to Ely D 55 5
Canterbury - BLs around B 58 9
Cardiff to Dowlais (Cae Harris) E 47 5
Cardiff to Pontypridd E 95 6
Cardiff to Swansea E 42 0
Carlisle to Hawick E 85 7
Carmarthen to Fishguard E 66 6
Caterham & Tattenham Corner B251
Central & Southern Spain NG E 91 8
Chard and Yeovil - BLs a C 30 7
Charing Cross to Dartford A 75 8
Charing Cross to Orpington A 96 3
Cheddar - Branch Line to B 90 9
Cheltenham to Andover C 43 7
Cheltenham to Redditch D 81 4
Chester to Rhyl E 93 2
Chichester to Portsmouth A 14 7
Clacton and Walton - BLs to F 04 8
Clapham Jn to Beckenham Jn B 36 7
Cleobury Mortimer - BLs a E 18 5
Clevedon & Portishead - BLs to D180
Colonel Stephens - His Empire D 62 3
Consett to South Shields E 57 4
Cornwall Narrow Gauge D 56 2
Corris and Vale of Rheidol E 65 9
Craven Arms to Llandeilo E 35 2
Craven Arms to Wellington E 33 8
Crawley to Littlehampton A 34 5
Cromer - Branch Lines around C 26 0
Croydon to East Grinstead B 48 0
Crystal Palace & Catford Loop B 87 1
Cyprus Narrow Gauge E 13 0

D
Darjeeling Revisited F 09 3
Darlington Leamside Newcastle E 28 4
Darlington to Newcastle D 98 2
Dartford to Sittingbourne B 34 3
Derwent Valley - BL to the D 06 7
Devon Narrow Gauge E 09 3
Didcot to Banbury D 02 9
Didcot to Swindon C 84 0
Didcot to Winchester C 13 0
Dorset & Somerset NG D 76 0
Douglas - Laxey - Ramsey E 75 8
Douglas to Peel C 88 8
Douglas to Port Erin C 55 0
Douglas to Ramsey D 39 5
Dover to Ramsgate A 78 9
Dublin Northwards in 1950s E 31 4
Dunstable - Branch Lines to E 27 7

E
Ealing to Slough C 42 0
East Cornwall Mineral Railways D 22 7
East Croydon to Three Bridges A 53 6
Eastern Spain Narrow Gauge E 56 7
East Grinstead - BLs a O 07 9
East London - Branch Lines of C 44 4
East London Line B 80 0
East of Norwich - Branch Lines E 69 7
Effingham Junction - BLs a A 74 1
Ely to Norwich C 90 1
Enfield Town & Palace Gates D 32 6
Epsom to Horsham A 30 7
Eritrean Narrow Gauge E 38 3
Euston to Harrow & Wealdstone C 89 5
Exeter to Barnstaple B 15 2
Exeter to Newton Abbot C 49 9
Exeter to Tavistock B 69 5
Exmouth - Branch Lines to B 00 8

F
Fairford - Branch Line to A 52 9
Falmouth, Helston & St. Ives C 74 1
Fareham to Salisbury A 67 3
Faversham to Dover B 05 3
Felixstowe & Aldeburgh - BL to D 20 3
Fenchurch Street to Barking C 20 8
Festiniog - 50 yrs of enterprise C 83 3
Festiniog 1946-55 E 01 7
Festiniog in the Fifties B 68 8
Festiniog in the Sixties B 91 6
Finsbury Park to Alexandra Pal C 02 8
Frome to Bristol B 77 0

G
Gloucester to Bristol D 35 7
Gloucester to Cardiff D 66 1
Gosport - Branch Lines around A 36 9
Greece Narrow Gauge D 72 2

H
Hampshire Narrow Gauge D 36 4
Harrow to Watford D 14 2
Harwich & Hadleigh - BLs to F 02 4
Hastings to Ashford A 37 6
Hawkhurst - Branch Line to A 66 6
Hayling - Branch Line to A 12 3
Hay-on-Wye - BL around D 92 0
Haywards Heath to Seaford A 28 4
Hemel Hempstead - BLs to D 88 3
Henley, Windsor & Marlow - BLa C77 2
Hereford to Newport D 54 8
Hertford & Hatfield - BLs a E 58 1
Hertford Loop E 71 0
Hexham to Carlisle D 75 3
Hexham to Hawick F 08 6
Hitchin to Peterborough D 07 4
Holborn Viaduct to Lewisham A 81 9
Horsham - Branch Lines to A 02 4
Huntingdon - Branch Line to A 93 2

I
Ilford to Shenfield C 97 0
Ilfracombe - Branch Line to B 21 3
Industrial Rlys of the South East A 09 3
Ipswich to Saxmundham C 41 3
Isle of Wight Lines - 50 yrs C 12 3
Italy Narrow Gauge F 17 8

K
Kent Narrow Gauge C 45 1
Kidderminster to Shrewsbury E 10 9
Kingsbridge - Branch Line to C 98 7
Kings Cross to Potters Bar E 62 8
Kingston & Hounslow Loops A 83 3
Kingswear - Branch Line to C 17 8

L
Lambourn - Branch Line to C 70 3
Launceston & Princetown - BLs C 19 2
Lewisham to Dartford A 92 5
Lines around Wimbledon B 75 6
Liverpool Street to Chingford D 01 2
Liverpool Street to Ilford C 34 5
Llandeilo to Swansea E 46 8
London Bridge to Addiscombe B 20 6
London Bridge to East Croydon A 58 1
Longmoor - Branch Line to A 41 3
Looe - Branch Line to C 22 2
Lowestoft - BLs around E 40 6
Ludlow to Hereford E 14 7
Lydney - Branch Lines around E 26 0
Lyme Regis - Branch Line to A 45 1
Lynton - Branch Line to B 04 6

M
Machynlleth to Barmouth E 54 3
Maesteg and Tondu Lines E 06 2
March - Branch Lines around B 09 1
Marylebone to Rickmansworth D 49 4
Melton Constable to Yarmouth Bch E031
Midhurst - Branch Lines of E 78 9
Midhurst - Branch Lines to F 00 0
Mitcham Junction Lines B 01 5
Mitchell & company C 59 8
Monmouth - Branch Lines to E 20 8
Monmouthshire Eastern Valleys D 71 5
Moretonhampstead - BL to C 27 7
Moreton-in-Marsh to Worcester D 26 5
Mountain Ash to Neath D 80 7

N
Newbury to Westbury C 66 6
Newcastle to Hexham D 69 2
Newport (IOW) - Branch Lines to A 26 0
Newquay - Branch Lines to C 71 0
Newton Abbot to Plymouth C 60 4
Newtown to Aberystwyth E 41 4
North East German NG D 44 9
Northern France Narrow Gauge C 75 8
Northern Spain Narrow Gauge E 83 3
North London Line B 94 7
North Woolwich - BLs around C 65 9

O
Ongar - Branch Line to E 05 5
Oswestry - Branch Lines around E 60 4
Oswestry to Whitchurch E 81 9
Oxford to Bletchley D 57 9
Oxford to Moreton-in-Marsh D 15 9

P
Paddington to Ealing C 37 6
Paddington to Princes Risborough C819
Padstow - Branch Line to B 54 1
Peterborough to Kings Lynn E 32 1
Plymouth - BLs around B 98 5
Plymouth to St. Austell C 63 5
Pontypool to Mountain Ash D 65 4
Pontypridd to Merthyr F 14 7
Pontypridd to Port Talbot E 86 4
Porthmadog 1954-94 - BLa B 31 2
Portmadoc 1923-46 - BLa B 13 8
Portsmouth to Southampton A 31 4
Portugal Narrow Gauge E 67 3
Potters Bar to Cambridge D 70 8
Princes Risborough - BL to D 05 0
Princes Risborough to Banbury C 85 7

R
Reading to Basingstoke B 27 5
Reading to Didcot C 79 6
Reading to Guildford A 47 5
Redhill to Ashford A 73 4
Return to Blaenau 1970-82 C 64 2
Rhyl to Bangor F 15 4
Rhymney & New Tredegar Lines E 48 2
Rickmansworth to Aylesbury D 61 6
Romania & Bulgaria NG E 23 9
Romneyrail C 32 1
Ross-on-Wye - BLs around E 30 7
Ruabon to Barmouth E 84 0
Rugby to Birmingham E 37 6
Rugby to Loughborough F 12 3
Rugby to Stafford F 07 9
Ryde to Ventnor A 19 2

S
Salisbury to Westbury B 39 8
Saxmundham to Yarmouth C 69 7
Saxony Narrow Gauge D 47 0
Seaton & Sidmouth - BLs to A 95 6
Selsey - Branch Line to A 04 8
Sheerness - Branch Line to B 16 2
Shenfield to Ipswich E 96 3
Shrewsbury - Branch Line to A 86 4
Shrewsbury to Chester E 70 3
Shrewsbury to Ludlow E 21 5
Shrewsbury to Newtown E 29 1
Sierra Leone Narrow Gauge D 28 9
Sirhowy Valley Line E 12 3
Sittingbourne to Ramsgate A 90 1
Slough to Newbury C 56 7
South African Two-foot gauge E 51 2
Southampton to Bournemouth A 42 0
Southend & Southminster BLs E 76 5
Southern France Narrow Gauge C 47 5
South London Line B 46 6
South Lynn to Norwich City F 03 1
Southwold - Branch Line to A 15 4
Spalding - Branch Lines around E 52 9
St Albans to Bedford D 08 1
St. Austell to Penzance C 67 3
ST Isle of Wight A 56 7
Stourbridge to Wolverhampton E 16 1
St. Pancras to Barking D 68 5
St. Pancras to Folkestone E 88 8
St. Pancras to St. Albans C 78 9
Stratford-u-Avon to Birmingham D777
Stratford-u-Avon to Cheltenham C253
ST West Hants A 69 7
Sudbury - Branch Lines to F 19 2
Surrey Narrow Gauge C 87 1
Sussex Narrow Gauge C 68 0
Swanley to Ashford B 45 9
Swansea to Carmarthen E 59 8
Swindon to Bristol C 96 3
Swindon to Gloucester D 46 3
Swindon to Newport D 30 2
Swiss Narrow Gauge C 94 9

T
Talyllyn 60 E 98 7
Taunton to Barnstaple B 60 2
Taunton to Exeter C 82 6
Tavistock to Plymouth B 88 6
Tenterden - Branch Line to A 21 5
Three Bridges to Brighton A 35 2
Tilbury Loop C 86 4
Tiverton - BLs around C 62 8
Tivetshall to Beccles D 41 8
Tonbridge to Hastings A 44 4
Torrington - Branch Lines to B 37 4
Towcester - BLs around E 39 0
Tunbridge Wells BLs A 32 1

U
Upwell - Branch Line to B 64 0

V
Victoria to Bromley South A 98 7
Vivarais Revisited E 08 6

W
Wantage - Branch Line to D 25 8
Wareham to Swanage 50 yrs D098
Waterloo to Windsor A 54 3
Waterloo to Woking A 38 3
Watford to Leighton Buzzard D 45 6
Welshpool to Llanfair E 49 9
Wenford Bridge to Fowey C 09 3
Westbury to Bath B 55 8
Westbury to Taunton C 76 5
West Cornwall Mineral Rlys D 48 7
West Croydon to Epsom B 08 4
West German Narrow Gauge D 93 7
West London - BLs of C 50 5
West London Line B 84 8
West Wiltshire - BLs of D 12 8
Weymouth - BLs A 65 9
Willesden Jn to Richmond B 71 8
Wimbledon to Beckenham C 58 1
Wimbledon to Epsom B 62 6
Wimborne - BLs around A 97 0
Wisbech - BLs around C 01 7
Witham & Kelvedon - BLs a E 82 6
Woking to Alton A 59 8
Woking to Portsmouth A 25 3
Woking to Southampton A 55 0
Wolverhampton to Shrewsbury E444
Worcester to Birmingham D 97 5
Worcester to Hereford D 38 6
Worthing to Chichester A 06 2

Y
Yeovil - 50 yrs change C 38 3
Yeovil to Dorchester A 76 5
Yeovil to Exeter A 91 8